SOUL SURGE

DISCOVER YOUR POWER, CHANGE THE WORLD

JASMINE JUDSON

Contents

Introduction

I wrote this book because I was searching for it and couldn't find anything like it. There are so many creative, innovative, and beautiful books on self-reflection and empowerment out there, but as I was seeking a tool to help me navigate trying times with self-love in mind, they often fell short. I read some beautiful books, but the seemingly separate intellectual and creative sides of my brain craved a way to explore and heal my inner terrain in a way that honored my duality.

It's hard to know if I accomplished this incredible task; however, writing the book has helped me immensely. It has been a sweet journey and has shown me that we are capable of healing our hearts. If this book brings you hope and courage in trying times, it has served its purpose. My intention for each of us is that we find the serenity our souls are craving and discover our power so that we can change the world.

Who Am I?

I am a hetero, cisgender white woman born and raised in Maui, Hawaii. I left Hawaii at age 17. I traveled the world a bit, studied a bit, and learned a lot. I explored, loved, and lost before returning home some 15 years later to visit my family.

A chance meeting with the man who would later become my husband shifted the course of my world and started a chapter in my life that I consider to be one of the richest to date. My husband is an incredible man and one of my most treasured support systems. Many of my undertakings would not have been possible without him, and I hope that everyone finds a partner who respects, honors, and cherishes them the way we do in our relationship.

The positive impact my husband has had on my life is worthy of pages of eloquent prose honoring the way he has shown up for our relationship, but this is a book about cultivating a deeper relationship with oneself. The path to personal empowerment is one best taken individually, and I was only able to invite his love into my life after I had learned to love myself more.

Of course, you can be married or in a relationship to start this incredible work. Learning to love yourself more will fuse love into every aspect of your life, *especially* your romantic relationships. However, these romantic relationships can never be a replacement for the one you cultivate with yourself. Humans come and go, people will let you down, and seasons of friendship will change, but designing a synergistic relationship with yourself will ALWAYS yield personal benefits.

Due to my island upbringing and because I grew up in a large family, I have always loved being part of a community and creating opportunities for people to gather. Bringing people together for the greater good in some capacity or another was a giant part of the destiny I saw for myself. Although I had no idea of the magnitude in which I would commit myself to this goal, I chose to bring humans together through yoga studios and movement classes. They were based on the "self-healing practice" I created in my bedroom to recover after a toxic relationship unraveled. I chose to share it with the world when I opened my first yoga studio in July 2015.

I called this practice "ShaktiRize," a call to action for the divine feminine in all of us. On the surface, these classes are a combination of world dance, high-intensity interval training, and bumping bass. *SF Chronicle* did a feature and called it, "Somewhere between a spiritual Zumba and sexy Kundalini yoga." However, when you participate in a class, you discover it's so much more than just physical movement. It's a safe space for women-identifying humans to come together and celebrate their individuality as well as the collective part of the divine feminine. We break down barriers, push ourselves outside our comfort zones mentally and physically, and learn to love ourselves a little more in the presence of some fellow fierce phenomenal femme fatales.

Classes start with grounding and intention setting, proceed to a seated warm up, and progress to expressive dance. For 60-75 minutes, we move with one another as we remember our strengths and forget our shortcomings. For many of us, the space we create is our safe place, and the practice is our saving grace. As the women lay on their mats in piles of sweat, smiles, and tears after class, I speak to the group. The words pour out of my soul and into the room. They come from my mouth, but are never planned in my mind. It's different every time, and the words never seem to fail me.

Even when I was the only person practicing ShaktiRize from the confines of my bedroom, I always concluded each session with a mental rundown of self-affirmations. As I'll explain later in the book, I was a bit broken when I found my way into this kind of movement. When I completed a session, I would lay on my mat in tears and whisper words of love and encouragement to myself.

I still don't know exactly where these post-practice words come from. I never write anything down before class. I simply quiet my mind, listen to my heart, and share what surfaces. I like to think the women in my classes create these words, that we are so interconnected that these meditations are a co-creation of our collective. I share something different after each class, never to be shared again. Often, women ask me what I was reading after class and where they could read those words again. I feel both humbled and grateful that universal energy moves through me in this way. I jokingly call it my superpower and am thankful that I can help even a single person in my classes and life. It is a great gift, and I don't take it lightly.

I started to write this book in 2019 after a few of my incredible students encouraged me to put pen to paper on some of the rapid-stream thoughts I spontaneously share after each class. In many ways, these class musings were things I wanted someone else to say to me, but I quickly realized that many of the lessons of love and loss I wanted to hear were universally craved. What started as a fun side project for me in 2019 morphed into a survival tool in 2020.

Everyone on the planet has been affected in some way by the Coronavirus pandemic. In that way, we have never been so interconnected. There has never been a time where we have all simultaneously experienced some version of a common narrative. But of course, that is where the commonalities splinter. Some of us lost businesses and dreams, while others lost incomes, homes, or the ability to feed their families. Still others lost loved ones or even their own lives. There has never been a MORE IMPORTANT time for us to come together for the greater good of humanity and our planet.

The global pandemic was, and is, a heartbreaker. The relentlessness of these years has persisted even amongst our cries for mercy. These years taught me about love and loss in a way that was unlike any others.

In 2015, I opened my first yoga studio. In 2020, I closed three of my four locations. My story is not uncommon. Even in the midst of my loss, I understood I was among the fortunate ones who still had something sacred to hold onto.

My studios were always so much more than businesses to me. They were like my children, and every member felt like family. I loved them deeply and nurtured them with every fiber of my being. What took years to nourish and grow was decimated in a matter of weeks. I am still grappling with what it all means from a universal and spiritual perspective. I may never fully understand it. What I can say is that only through that year of extreme loss was I able to dive a bit deeper into a place of extreme gratitude and even hope. I suspect the two are intrinsically interconnected. Only through loss can the heart truly experience love. Magic is discovered only through countless mistakes. The wounds encountered from being human brew an individual blend of wisdom.

From the initial (and I assumed temporary) closing of my four studios, to the permanent closing of one and then three locations, I journeyed through many incantations of self and discovered a duality in me that has become my greatest treasure. The darkest of shadows and the brightest of lights make up the human experience. My deeper dive into self created the safe space I had been seeking.

Inside you is a place you can go that has the tools you need to heal your every ailment. This place is always available to you, but it takes some conjuring to find the path.

When my heart was breaking, I wasn't entirely sure I could (or wanted to) continue. Everything hurt, all the time. Each day was a journey of pain as I navigated loss and tried to get back to a personal place of joy. I searched everywhere for tools to help me move through my sorrow more quickly. While I still believe time is the universal healer of all wounds, I also know when your heart is breaking (due to loss of a business or loss of a loved one), time can be the cruelest of companions.

What You Will Learn

What is *your* intention in picking up this book? What are you ready to shift? What would you like to call to yourself? What would you love to leave behind?

Just a warning: this book will forever change the way you view yourself and the world around you. It will shake up what you know to be "true" about your life and replace it with the authenticity you deserve and the purpose you crave. From this newfound authenticity, you can step into a place of power that can help you to be of service to our sweet world. If this is NOT what you want, put.the.book.down. Don't turn another page. Continue living your safe life and continue experiencing varying degrees of happiness. I wish you only the best, and I hope you find what you are seeking. However, if you know, deep down, that you are here for so much more than the life that you are leading, if you know and trust that you are meant to authentically support and love other humans, and if your soul is screaming for some way to share itself in service, you are on the right track.

Who Is this Book For?

I seek to actively participate and include people from a variety of backgrounds in my day-to-day existence. However, the work I do is primarily focused on supporting and nurturing the feminine. I wrote this book from my own limited perspective and sought diversity coaches along the way to be as inclusive and welcoming to men, trans people, and gender-neutral humans who are looking to tap more deeply into the feminine in self.

So often we want to assign a gender role to our feminine and masculine energies, which unnecessarily simplifies the beautiful complexities of being human. Everyone has both masculine and feminine qualities, and this book should feel like a safe space for those who read it. I attempted to keep my wording as gender neutral as possible in most of the book so as to not exclude anyone from being invited to participate. However, this book is ultimately about tapping into the wild warrior woman who resides within, in whatever form she takes. I am grateful in advance for your willingness to see me for my intention. Take what you can from this work, and leave the rest behind.

For my courageous sisters, those of you who are ready to dive head-first into the center of you: take a deep breath and get into it! It won't always be easy, but it will always be good. I promise you, you are worth all the time and energy you pour into yourself with the greater good in mind. Let yourself blossom and bloom under your own tutelage. Trust that the internal work you are doing will allow you to better do the external work that needs to be done.

You are worth it, and the world needs conscious, humble leaders who have chosen to step up for the greater good. Dive in and work on yourself, but never forget WHY. When you learn to love yourself more every day, you will have so much more to give the world.

I am deeply honored and so excited to be on this journey with you. Thank you for the privilege of your time and your willingness to do your part to create change.

The Purpose of this Book

The tools in this book will help you create your heart's own roadmap to freedom and love. Once discovered, you will soar from your newfound place of love. As your soul ascends, you will be able to positively serve not only your family and community, but also our sweet, sweet planet.

Being human means that at one point in the future, if it hasn't already, the bottom will suddenly drop out of your life. You will find yourself in an inexplicably different situation than hours or days before, and you won't know how to pick up the pieces of what remains to create some semblance of wholeness for yourself. When this happens, my greatest wish is for you to dive head-first into yourself and find the strength and courage you need to continue with your head held high. Inside you is a spark that can ignite the fires of your passions and will help you rise from the ashes like the phoenix you are.

This book serves as a reminder, to empower you to go deeper into your knowledge of self. Your exploration of self-love will extinguish the old beliefs that no longer serve you. Only from a place of deep understanding of your heart's inner workings can you truly be of service to everyone you meet. There is no nobler goal, nor one that is more aligned with your soul's purpose, than to create an authentic life, and then share yourself in all your authenticity with the world.

While this may not always be easy, it will be worth it. This book is part personal exploration and part personal introspection. In an effort to walk the walk and practice what I preach, I have shared some of my own journey with you. From my own experience, I know it's not easy. Some days, I wanted to fold into myself and disappear forever.

When you are navigating a challenging time, other people may want to support you, but ONLY YOU can find the answers to your salvation.

It's all inside you. Your soul's deepest purpose and your heart's innermost desires lie carefully protected in your internal vault. Once you forge the key from the fires of your life's challenges, you unlock your magical innerworkings, and discover how much you have to give the world. Once unlocked, the treasures and life tools in that vault are yours to keep forever.

You will never need to depend on another person for love or freedom. Each relationship you CHOOSE to enter is a gift, and one that adds more value to your existence. You will align yourself with your purpose, and by doing so, you can more fully share yourself with the world. That is the sweetest gift you can give. It is your responsibility to share yourself with the world whenever you can, especially if you come from a place of beautiful privilege.

As you feel your emotions, be sure to honor them and have patience with yourself. You process experiences in a different way than others, and it is important to properly embrace the individuality of self-expression during this time.

As an individual, you are amazing, but when you partner with others, together you can create lasting, positive change. This is an incredible time of growth and progress socially and personally; women are at the forefront of this movement, playing an extremely vital role in the process of building bright futures. YOU are a crucial component of this incredible change at this unparalleled time. There is so much magic in you, and it needs to be shared with the world! Your future is in your hands; create one that fills your heart with the joy of being you and then PLEASE share it!

1

Diving into Your Depths

Our society doesn't necessarily support emotional or spiritual depth. In a world of Instagram reels, instant gratification, and (not quite) reality television, we are rarely celebrated for taking the time to go deeper. Society wants us to crave the quick, superficial fix of dopamine we get from a Facebook like or new Instagram follower. We are celebrated more for the fancy car we drive and the number of dollars in that bank account, than the time and energy we spend on helping the planet or becoming a better person. Aren't you craving more? Isn't your soul longing to surge into the depths of who you truly are?

Mine was.

Ten years ago, though I didn't recognize it at the time, I was a liar.

I had always been told that I was "fun, confident, and outgoing." I had many friends and felt well-liked in my circles. I heard these reflections often enough that I believed them to be true. I was a fun person who people loved to be around. I never questioned these assumptions because I knew these words were positive and indicative of who I wanted to be. I told myself that confident and outgoing women were always loved, and if I was always loved, then I would never be alone.

I never took the time to question whether this narrative was true, or if I even wanted to be "loved" for such superficial qualities. I never needed to. In this previous phase of my life, I viewed myself as confident, well-liked, and outgoing. I had tons of friends, was invited to all the parties, and knew the DJs by name. But deep down, I was lying to myself. I was riddled with insecurities and *so desperate for love* that I sometimes found it in places that were less than lovable.

My default process in a relationship was this: whoever liked me enough to pursue me the most got to be my boyfriend for a period of between one and five years. May the best man (or at least the most obsessive one) win. I wasn't concerned with finding someone who would tend to my profound insecurities or invite me to dive deeper into self. I just wanted someone who would adore me for the identity I had created. I had built a very superficial relationship with myself, so it's no surprise that the friendships and romantic relationships I drew into my world perpetuated that lack of depth. I just wanted to have fun and for someone to tell me I was pretty.

I don't recommend choosing your romantic relationships this way.

I didn't intentionally pursue a person who spoke to my soul and ignited my heart. I wasn't even aware of what my heart desired and my soul craved. I had never gone that deep with myself before, and certainly never sought that in a romantic counterpart.

I didn't realize it at the time, but every human we encounter has the ability to enhance or detract from our life force with every interaction. Our roommates, friends, families, and romantic partners all influence the way we perceive ourselves. If we only surround ourselves with superficial party friends, then we will see only that energy reflected back on us. There is a constant duality of light and dark that exists at all times around us, and we get to choose which of those forces we desire to partake in. Our relationships are merely mirrors for what we want to see, and unless we are clear on what our souls are craving, we may find we unintentionally open ourselves to dark and toxic forces.

This was only part of the reason I ended up in a relationship with Devland (not his real name). The initial attraction was to the darkness I saw in him. It seemed exciting, intriguing, and dangerous. My previous relationships had all been so light-hearted and easy; we never fought, but we never went deeper. We danced on Saturday nights, brunched on Sundays, and kept our conversations focused on the superficial. With Devland, it felt different. I mistook his damage for depth, and it almost swallowed me whole. I won't get into the depths of that relationship, but I will share something I wrote years after it ended when I was able to come to terms with what it had been:

When I think about him, I can't sleep.

He texts me witty one-liners that spark my interest and bring butterflies rushing to my stomach. He has a laugh that's childlike, but he drinks whiskey like a champ. The juxtaposition of this man-child has my inner mother and my inner whore competing for his affection. He takes me to the most beautiful places...inner and external landscapes that move me to tears...the good kind. How can there be so much beauty in the world that I am just now discovering? He lights me up and shows me the hidden magic. I sparkle under his affections and the world responds in turn.

When I think about him, I can't sleep.

There is something dark and damaged that I can't define and I like it because it mirrors how dark and damaged I know I am. Two halves don't make a whole, but maybe we can pick up the broken pieces of our lives and build something beautiful: a mosaic of church cathedral stained glass windows that heal every sin we've ever committed and those of our fathers too. There is a special place in hell for our kind. He and I both know that secret and understand what a bitter relief that brings.

When I think about him, I can't sleep.

My eyes are raw and my throat is swollen from the tears. It's late, I'm alone, and he's not answering his phone. Maybe he's with her, or her, or her. A sea of sirens washes the shores of my barren life with salt water, in the sweat on our sheets and the tears in my eyes that can't meet the gaze of my dearest friends. They don't understand. We have something that transcends the mundane... something that transcends the world...only through the pain can I truly live. The suffering makes me feel alive and speaks to a part of my soul that has never known voices. One night we take mushrooms and I realize he's the devil, here to eat me alive. And I stay. I hate myself and I wonder how I got here, but my life makes no sense without him.

When I think about him, I can't sleep.

This is all my fault, he says, and I know that I'm broken, and fucked up, and I feel so brittle, like the top layer of the beach when it's been beaten down by the sun. You can remove just that crinkled top layer, and if you are careful you can hold it in your hand and it won't break. I'm so ready to break, but the world won't let me go. I beg for peace. I fill my nights with whiskey bottles, stolen cigarettes, and no food. Daylight is a secret torture as it's meant for the living, but the sun refuses to believe I'm already dead. If I can just fix this, I will heal all the wounds before him and all the wounds after him. People are worried for me. We share a shuttle home from the bar with a random couple one night and they know something is wrong. She tells me I can come with them, that I don't deserve this, that I'll be safe with her. I think she's an angel, a beacon of light. She must not realize I already belong to the darkness. I ignore her pleas and let the devil walk me home. He says he's the only one who knows the way.

When I think about him, I can't sleep.

My tummy is in knots and it may be days or weeks since I've last eaten. I question my sanity and think I may have dreamed the woman I was before. She traveled the world alone, took risks, and didn't take shit from anyone. She was so fucking funny and laughed easily. Where did she go? She feels like a mirage I created for something real to hold onto in this time of torture. I don't want to hold on anymore. I want to die. I walk through the world like a ghost and wonder if maybe I've already died and have found myself in purgatory. How anyone can be happy escapes me. How can there be so much pain and sorrow in the world that I am just now discovering? I feel all the black and the ugly in my heart, and my head, and my shoulders where he didn't mean to hold me too hard against the wall. I bruise so easily now.

It's been years, but sometimes he still haunts my dreams. I wake with saltwater in my eyes and in my bed. Even now, when I think about him, I can't sleep.

They were challenging and dark years and they ripped me apart. The relationship had started out as a dream, but it quickly became a nightmare. When I found my way out of it, I was a mess. I felt mangled, bruised, and a shadow of my former self. All my innermost fears and deepest demons had bubbled their way to the surface. I believed at the time that I had been permanently broken. My closest friends and family members could offer no solace or comfort. I felt totally alone. Their words of support and encouragement fell to the floor before they reached my heart. I felt impenetrable and beyond repair. No one could provide me with the support I needed. Couldn't they see that I was dying inside, a wisp of the woman I once was?

What I didn't realize at the time was that I wasn't broken. Instead, I'd been broken open, and was about to bear witness to some of the most incredible resilience and magic that resided within me. This relationship was merely the catalyst for my soul to surge.

The Value in Suffering

Priests, saints, and healers of all modalities have understood the necessity of overcoming obstacles to step into a place of infinite and divine potential. They acknowledge a beauty that blossoms when we circumnavigate suffering and struggle. Like a literal birthing, it is messy and painful; it challenges us to our very core, and then it challenges us even more. Such is life, and without these wounds, we would never be able to tap into our infinite wisdom. The wound contains the wisdom.

John of the cross speaks of a dark night of the soul, a period when you feel completely separated from your own divinity and the light of a power much greater than yourself. It's a lonely and individualized journey where the only thing left to do is to surrender to learning to love and trust yourself in a way you never needed to before. It becomes a necessity for survival. It is new, it is scary, and it strips you raw.

In the movie of your life, this is a self-love story about you and yourself. In this scene of the film (and your life), we aren't sure if the relationship is going to make it or not. Watching from the outside on the big screen, the obstacle may not seem as important as the weight it is given by the characters engaging in the conflict. To the audience, it seems like it should be so easy to solve this simple conundrum and get back to a place of peace.

This is also true for the dilemmas of our own lives. As we are living them, we hold the weight of the world on our shoulders while the world turns on, seemingly oblivious to our pain and struggle. It is personal, and anyone outside of the relationship can not possibly grasp its weight or its importance. Which is why we must learn to do the work on our own.

The Dark Night of the Soul

When I walked away from my relationship with Devland, I wasn't sure who I was anymore. This "confident" woman was afraid to sleep in a bed by herself. This "outgoing" human was terrified to hop on a plane without a companion. I had moved to Italy at 19, ALONE, without knowing anyone or speaking the language, but now I didn't even think I could take a bus to the next town by myself. Fear consumed me in every aspect of my life.

I was a ghost, wandering through the land of the living, and no one seemed to notice. I remember distinctly wondering how people could laugh and smile when there was such a deep capacity for suffering inside me.

I knew I had to dive inside myself and find the root of the wound that was bringing me down. The relationship with Devland was only a reflection of how I viewed myself and what I thought I deserved. When I escaped the relationship, in a matter of weeks I realized that to enter something so toxic, there had to be a big part of me that didn't truly love myself. Only by finding that place of personal love would I ever truly be free or healed.

The thought terrified me.

I didn't know how to heal from past trauma, and I certainly hadn't done a very good job of loving myself in the present. I was SURE I was going to attempt this personal work, and when I did I was going to die. I don't even mean in a metaphorical way. I honestly felt I would dive into some of these questions and they would break me, that I would cross over into some dark, soulless void and never return. (I may or may not have a flair for the dramatic.)

My sweet sister, if you are currently in an abusive or toxic relationship, know that you are not weak or unlovable. There is so much you can share with the world if you allow yourself to remember the strength you had months or years ago. This experience showed me that I didn't enter into a toxic relationship overnight. I gave up my power day by day and moment by moment until I woke up one morning and didn't even recognize myself in the mirror. So many of us have been stolen from in the name of love.

As women, we are socialized to "compromise" in relationships; everyone tells us they are hard work and won't always be easy. But check in to see what you are compromising. A compromise in a healthy relationship might look like having Indian food one night and Thai food the other, to accommodate differing tastes. A compromise should never mean you put aside your safety (emotionally, physically, mentally, OR spiritually) to appease another person. A compromise in a healthy relationship won't strip you of your confidence, joy, or health.

It takes courage to remove yourself from any situation that does not serve you. Have faith in a future you can't even imagine. It is more peaceful and abundant than your mind can comprehend. Be open to unimaginable, magical possibilities that could exist in your future. I thought this relationship was the end of me, but it was truly just the beginning. Long no more, sweetheart, *you* are the one you have been waiting for.

If you are in a relationship that is jeopardizing you in any way, here is a resource that can help:

National Domestic Violence Hotline

Provides national and local resources and support 24/7.
https://www.thehotline.org/
Call 1.800.799.SAFE (7233)
TTY 1.800.787.3224

I had to make a decision. I knew if I didn't create a safe and loving space for myself on the inside, I was never going to find that relationship externally from me. Yes, my previous relationship was toxic, but why had I chosen to stay in that place? Why did I choose friends who would party with me but never help me move? Why did I crave popularity when I was really seeking something much more profound? These musings sparked a personal exploration that brought me my greatest tools for self love. My hope is that by sharing these with you, you too can find your way out of seemingly hopeless situations into a place of deep, personal power.

Start Today, Start with You

Over the course of this book, you will have time to dive into the sweet spots of yourself. I have included real talk questions and exercises after each chapter to invite you to go deeper into a place of pure, personal exploration. This place is where all your magic resides, and it is important work.

However, you never want to lose sight of the reasons you are showing up. Yes, the internal work heals old wounds and taps into new sources of power, and this is vital. But, don't stop there. You'll need this power to combat systems of oppression and show up for humans who may not be as fortunate as you are. It's all interconnected. When you show up for the planet and its people, you are building a world you want to live in, and you lay a foundation for future generations to continue on this path with greater success. Show up for yourself, then show up for the world.

Step outside your comfort zone (if you know me personally, you know this is definitely my MO). You may travel to places that will feel a bit foreign, a bit icky, and maybe even a bit scary. I promise you, this is work I have first been willing to do myself, and I am never done. It is an ongoing journey, a peeling back of layers to uncover the brilliance that resides within. It is not always easy, but it is always good. It is time to come together to create a global shift. Start today, start with you.

Real Talk Questions:

Take a moment to ponder these questions, and then write your answers directly in this book.

Yes, in the book.

All of you rule-following femmes are already getting a beautiful taste of defying expectations of the status quo. Now take that pen and write in the freaking book.

Extra Credit: Tap into the creativity of your Sacral Chakra[1] center and grab all of your favorite colored pencils or paints and make this place

---

1   The Sacral Chakra is located two inches below your belly button and is responsible for creativity, sexuality, and self-expression.

into art. Color in the margins, doodle in the borders, and create a beautiful, vibrant masterpiece out of this book that is reflective of your own magic and exquisiteness.

Please note: If you do not own this book, you should write your answers in a separate place. Reading on an ereader? Buy a beautiful notebook for yourself to document this part of your evolution. It will become a manifesto for yourself that will change as you do. It will contain all the sentiments your heart is longing to receive. My intention is that this book becomes a journal of your heart's deepest desires, and a love letter to the most sacred parts of your soul.

Real Talk Questions:

Which of your relationships support the most authentic version of you? Which of your relationships support an identity you long to embody? Do those identities support your personal growth and evolution?

_____

_____

_____

_____

Which of your relationships no longer serve you and the woman you are becoming? Which of your relationships are toxic? How would it feel like to no longer interact with these people?

_____

_____

_____

_____

_____

How can you shift the narrative of your perception of certain relationships to create greater freedom and growth in self?

_____

_____

_____

_____

_____

_____

What lies do you tell yourself about "who you are?" How do these lies limit a more profound exploration of self?

_____

_____

_____

_____

_____

_____

In what ways do you let yourself down? What small steps can you take TODAY to better love and support yourself?

_____

_____

_____

_____

_____

_____

How can you show yourself more kindness TODAY?

_____

_____

_____

_____

_____

_____

2

Choosing a REAL-ATIONSHIP with Self

People let you down. Lovers betray you, friends flake out, and family members disappoint. The cast of characters in the movie of your life is forever shifting, yet you remain the ONLY true constant in your world. From your first breath until your last, you will always be with you. But being *with* yourself is drastically different than being THERE for yourself. Any time you seek validation and proof of worthiness outside yourself, you are setting yourself up to be seriously disappointed.

So often we seek love and a sense of belonging from outside sources, which is always a path to unhappiness. It's fine to cultivate and nurture relationships with the people we care about, but these connections can never take the place of the connection we must have with ourselves. Your relationship with yourself is THE most important one you can nurture. As a sweet bonus, once you have built and nourished a lifelong love affair with self, all your other relationships will be strengthened and enhanced. It's truly a win-win.

Trying to fill an internal void with external love and gratification is a recipe for disaster. It's like attempting to feed your body with printed-out pictures of food rather than a meal; your hunger will never be satiated, and it will always leave a bad taste in your mouth.

A lover may bring short-term joy and excitement, maybe even for years, but without the grounding force of a nourished relationship with yourself, you will experience long term suffering and heartache. You may be able to postpone the inevitable, but you cannot evade it forever.

You cannot hide from yourself, only delay the meeting, and in the process you attract other fragmented humans who have refused to face themselves as well. In this case, two halves DO NOT make a whole. Two broken people make for a lot of jagged edges, which is both a safety hazard to your heart and a liability to your soul. How can your soul surge if you are drowning in other people's wild and unpredictable seas?

Discovering your soul's limitless capacity requires that you dive into this human experience head-first and discover what is lying just beneath the surface: an ocean of truth and beauty. Only by taking the plunge into the difficult and the devastating can you truly discover the vastness of your courage. In that courage is your most authentic self, and therein lies your magic.

How I Found My Way Back

I hope that by sharing my story, I will save you some sorrow, but if you are as stubborn as me, you will likely need to navigate these lessons at your own time and pace. Maybe you already have.

My healing journey, like most, was non-linear. The first few months were make-or-break for me. Some days I felt better than I had felt in years. Other days I felt like death was at my door. Healing through a heartbreak, or the loss of something held dear, never has a direct pathway.

I wasn't sure how to move forward. I knew I wanted my heart to stop hurting, and I knew I needed to love myself unconditionally. I had a feeling those two were interconnected, and If I took a moment to be honest with myself, I knew I had the tools inside me. I needed to come back to the practices that had helped me in the past and create some space in my body and mind for healing.

Body movement and bass-bumping music are not the only ways to tap into the energy of the soul, but they are most assuredly my favorite ways. In addition, meditation and nature have always healed my heart and nurtured my soul, even in the most trying of times. Although I had been practicing yoga and meditating throughout my life, I knew I needed to invest more of myself into these practices if I wanted to get more out of them.

I began by meditating every day for at least 20 minutes. Some days I spent 20 minutes crying on my bed with meditation music playing, and some days I drifted into the spirit realm of peace with my higher self. I practiced yoga every day for at least a few minutes. Some days, child's pose[2] or savasana[3] were all I could muster. Other days, I played my favorite music and moved on my mat for hours. I tried to embrace my own duality in this healing process and life, finding gratitude that I can be so many things in my one single being even though my juxtaposed nature has caused me many moments of difficulty.

Committing to a daily meditation practice meant I was constantly on the search for new ways to harness my mind and emotions and use them for my greater good. During this time, I discovered a series of chakra[4] healing and cleansing meditations which introduced me to the very basics of Kundalini yoga.[5] It was exciting and refreshing to be able to create an altered state of being in my own mind and heart just through breathwork[6] and body movement. Although I had loved and practiced yoga for many years, Kundalini yoga felt very different. Something about the strange movements and repetition felt trance-like. It reminded me of when I lived in San Francisco and would go to big warehouse parties. I would dance in a room for HOURS with my eyes closed, letting my

---

2   Child's pose, also known as balasana, is a resting pose that stretches the lower back, improves circulation, and reduces anxiety.

3   Also known as Corpse pose, Savasana is the final pose in almost every yoga session. To do savasana, lay down flat on your back, with your arms at your side, and breathe evenly.

4   The chakras are the seven centers of spiritual power located throughout the body.

5   Kundalini yoga is associated with the divine feminine and seeks to activate the kundalini, located at the base of the spine.

6   Breathwork is the practice of using conscious breathing to improve physical, spiritual, or mental health.

body move however it chose without thinking. It is a freedom that is as close to divinity as I have ever felt.

Until this point, I had decided I couldn't even look at myself in the mirror. I hated everything about my body and the way I looked. I felt like I had been forever ruined by all the places Devland had touched. I cringed every time I saw my reflection in the mirror. Who was this weak, worthless, and feeble creature staring back at me? She was so thin, with dark circles under her eyes and an uncertainty in the way she moved that I had never seen. My reflection was a constant reminder of how far I had fallen from my former self, and I hated it.

I covered all the mirrors in my tiny studio apartment with sarongs. If, by chance, one of the sarongs dared to reveal a section of mirror, I was quick to return it to its covered state.

Despising oneself takes effort too.

One morning changed it all. Picture this:

I am practicing yoga in my bedroom. It's early morning, but the day has already started to heat up the single-ply construction of my plantation-style dwelling. I am wearing boy cut cotton panties and a sports bra, and I am already sweating. On this day, I have chosen to replace my standard downtempo playlist with some of my favorite old school hip hop and trance music tracks. I am in a downward facing dog listening to the music building in my headphones. I travel forward to a forward fold and sweep up to standing as the music crescendos.

My eyes are closed and I recall those many nights dancing in the dark interiors of San Francisco warehouses as the beat drops and moves me. I succumb to the desire and allow my body to swirl, turn, and fold into itself.

I am 19 again, grooving through the streets of Florence, Italy on my bike. I am 23 again, weaving my way through music festivals, making new friends. I am unbroken and beautiful. I am 28 again. I feel great pride receiving my letter of acceptance to medical school. My heart feels whole and free, and the world belongs to me.

I dance furiously for what feels like a lifetime...but it may have only been minutes. When I open my eyes, I see that the sarong has slipped away from its home covering the mirror, and I am completely revealed.

Beads of sweat drip down my body, and my hair is a tangled mess. My upper body heaves as I catch my breath and take myself in. Tears stream down my face as I see myself for the first time in a long time. I am a little girl, I am an ancient woman, I am old and young and broken and new. I am beautiful.

I cry for that woman in the mirror...the one I let down. When did I stop loving her? Have I ever really loved her? I ache for the little girl I used to be who always felt so sad and alone.

For that brief moment in time that feels like an eternity, I stare straight into my eyes and see my soul self, the self that extends beyond a body, or a job, or a relationship, or a moment. The soul that I am for all of this life and the lives before and after too.

In this moment in front of the mirror, I think I understand for an instant the magnitude of what this life has to offer. As humans we suffer, we love, we laugh, we desire, we learn, and we die. Days in pain seem like an eternity and moments of magic seem but an instant. However, our entire life, with all its complicated emotions, trials, tribulations, and triumphs, is truly less than a nanosecond in the energetic timeline of the universe.

At that moment, I knew I was one with it all. I was on my own individual journey, and yet simultaneously my journey contained a part of the bigger, universal picture.

In my studio apartment on that fateful morning, I was bared to myself, and I didn't look away. The music played loudly through my headphones, and I continued to dance and move and shake and I didn't look away. I bore witness to my beautiful, imperfect body that had been loved by some and mistreated by others and I didn't look away. I moved to reclaim it from anyone and everyone who had stolen it from me and I faced myself head on.

I had been so many things to so many people, but I had never been me just for me. In the mirror, moving in time to the music, I looked at myself deep into my own eyes and refused to look away. Song after song after song, I stayed committed to this newfound moving meditation before I fell into a pool of sweat and tears on my mat. Exhausted. Liberated. New.

At that moment, I felt called to be kind to myself for the first time in a very long time. I had been seeking a friend and an ally outside myself. I was craving words of support and wisdom that no one else could share with me. I knew exactly what I needed to hear.

I started to speak softly, "You are beautiful. You are whole. Nothing that has been done to you can ever take away from that wholeness. There is a magic inside of you that is only beginning to grow. Release your fear. Release your doubts and insecurities and surrender to the knowledge that every heartache and every tear was leading you to this exact moment in time. Put your faith back in yourself. You are not damaged or broken beyond repair. You are at the precipice of a new beginning."

I don't know where those words came from that day, and I don't know how I stumbled upon one of the greatest healing tools of my existence. Perhaps my many nights of tearful prayers were answered in this way. On that day, I saw the first ray of sunshine in my cloudy world. Whatever it was, I am eternally grateful. I stripped the sarongs from the mirrors that day, and even though I didn't know it at the time (or have a name for it until many months later), ShaktiRize was born.

I am so grateful for this dark and challenging period in my life. It was necessary to kindle the passionate fire of purpose I would need for my next chapter, a chapter that would require me to be the light in my world to guide me back home. I had to set my life on fire to see how truly bright those flames can burn.

I don't regret any of the challenges my life has shared because they brought new gifts and wisdom to my world in the form of lessons. I do wish I had heard more narratives that celebrate how transformational being single can be. I wish I could have understood that BECAUSE of (not in spite of) my perceived inconsistencies, I was a prize worthy of someone who rose to the occasion, who could nurture my body and heart at every shape and size.

I'm glad I know it now, but my hope is that by sharing my story, someone else will benefit in some small way. Like Ralph Waldo Emerson says, "To leave the world a bit better, whether by a healthy child, a garden patch, or a redeemed social condition; to know that even one life has breathed easier because you have lived—that is to have succeeded."

That's one of my stories, but my stories do not define me. Nor do your stories define you, or any of the things that have transpired in your life. We are not these bodies, and we are not these jobs. We are sweet souls on a stardust journey here on this planet for a specific reason. Yogis call it dharma. It is our reason for existing. It is our purpose. We all have one, and it is divine. The sooner we dive into our purpose, the happier and more aligned in our own lives we become.

"Out of suffering have emerged the strongest Souls; the most massive characters are seared with scars."

—Khalil Gibran

Real Talk Questions:

How do you speak to yourself? Are there phrases you need to eliminate from your conversation with yourself to be a bit more kind?

_____

_____

_____

_____

_____

_____

Do you ever pretend to be something you are not? How does that show up in your life?

_____

_____

_____

_____

_____

How has this altered identity served or stymied you?

_____

_____

_____

_____

_____

If you were to be completely honest with yourself about EVERYTHING, how would that change your life? How would you feel?

_____

_____

_____

_____

_____

_____

How could you make yourself a more important priority in your own life?

_____

_____

_____

_____

_____

_____

What three practices could you implement this week to cultivate a deeper and more authentic relationship with yourself?

_____

_____

_____

_____

_____

_____

You are made of stardust. You are a miracle worker born for greatness. Give yourself permission to fully step into that power, and watch the beauty of your life unfold. Like a lotus blossoming from the muck that surrounds it, you too were destined to take all of your trials and tribulations and turn them into beautiful magic.

YOU are your soul's mate. **YOU** are your own treasure. Love **ALL** of who you are.

You are re-learning how to love yourself. You knew how to once. You shined brightly without inhibitions or limitations when you were a baby, but then you forgot. You received undesirable reflections from your peers, your family, and your community, and so you retracted into yourself.

You learned that you could be pretty...but not TOO pretty.

That you could be smart...but not TOO smart.

That you could be talented...as long as that talent didn't threaten anyone else.

It is much easier to make yourself small so as not to offend than to shine brightly for all to see and risk their reflections and judgments.

But you my dear, were blessed with a warrior's heart, and the courage of a queen. Take risks that bring you greater happiness. YOU ARE WORTH IT!

Remember, not everyone will be happy with your success. Other people may be intimidated by your bright light. Shine anyway!

You, in your power, are so necessary for the world to prosper. In all of your strength and your glorious imperfections, you are changing our sweet world by being you. Choose that REAL-ationship with you. With compassion and kindness, remind yourself that if you are born with the strength to fall, you are also born with the courage to rise again.

3

Falling in Love

The romantic fantasy that is abundantly prevalent in our culture is the notion that there is someone out there in the world, your "ONE," who will complete you and make you whole when you are together. For some, this fantasy is ingrained so deeply they enter into relationships that don't serve or support them.

But you, my love, were born into wholeness, and whole you remain. Nothing and no one can strip away that wholeness without your permission. If somewhere along your journey you learned there was someone else who was going to come along and magically make you whole, you have given other people way too much power over your life's happiness.

You are the one you have been waiting for, your soul's mate and your heart's deepest longing! You never need to look outside yourself for love, acceptance, or happiness; you are complete. When someone comes along who loves and cherishes you for all the things you are and all the things you are not, you may find they are worthy of a bit more of your time. Maybe, at that point, the relationship will evolve and you will want to share the entirety of your life with them.

However, once you have re-discovered your own wholeness (it never left), you will never need to fill your emptiness with other people who don't care for your heart the way you deserve. You will have already nourished all your deepest aches and wounds and will come into the relationship as a whole, complete human. In that way, any romantic relationship, friendship, or acquaintance can be chosen with great care as it will need to *augment* the love you already have for yourself.

When in a relationship, it is more important to like yourself than to be liked. I'll say it again: **When in a relationship, it is more important to like yourself than to be liked.** This amplifies your internal voice and allows you to trust your own compass to choose what is right for you REGARDLESS of who shares the path with you.

IF you choose to add another human to your already amazing (and whole) life, you can change the way your counterparts show up by not settling for (and especially not competing for!) lackluster partners. There are some INCREDIBLE people in the world; caring, compassionate people with a deep internal strength. These people have the ability to rule side-by-side with royalty such as yourself. They are not intimidated by your successes, and are there to provide wisdom and support in times of need. These people EXIST and they are worth holding out for, the people who honor and cherish you for all the things you are and all the things you are not.

Let's create a world in which these partners are even more PLENTI-FUL. This REQUIRES that you DON'T settle for Mr. or Ms. "almost right." This means you have a deep love and respect for yourself that KNOWS you are worthy of a stellar partner because you are a superstar woman.

I get it, we all love attention. It feels GOOD to be seen as beautiful; it feels good to be acknowledged at a club with your friends. If you crave that attention, please, by all means, receive it. Enjoy it. But don't take it home and dress it up as your future spouse.

I have seen many women, beautiful, talented, intelligent women, set-tle for relationships that were inferior to them for many reasons because they didn't want to be alone. The partnerships were inferior not because of the amount of money they made or the job title they held. They were inferior because of the way they treated their mates; they were small-minded humans who sought to put down, belittle, and yes, sometimes abuse their partners. It is only a matter of time for a woman in this situation to forget she is a queen.

I know, because she was me.

I LOVED the attention. I pretended I didn't, and tried to appear modest, but I really loved it. It wasn't a good night for me if I went out with my girlfriends and not a single guy checked me out or flirted with me. I considered myself an independent woman so I would shut down 98% of the guys that approached me with a snappy comment or flippant remark, but heaven forbid they stopped approaching me. Desire and resistance. I understand now that I had not yet cultivated the relationship with myself that would sustain that craving. What was really lacking was MY attention...to me.

Our society encourages us to look externally for clues about who we are. We utilize social cues to determine whether we are pretty, smart, and worthy of love. We are conditioned from an early age to strive for these clues and cues. When we ask ourselves the question "Who am I?" undoubtedly a stream of belief systems will come to mind. These systems may not even be ours. Sometimes the belief systems people place on us aren't intended to limit us or hold us back. However, it is important we stay vigilant in our exploration of self by checking in from time to time to see if the things we KNOW about ourselves are still relevant..or even true. They may be beliefs we learned about ourselves from a young age when our parents unintentionally boxed us into the "You are pretty," "You are smart," "You are good at sports," or "You are shy." Society further boxed us in and segregated us by demanding, "Are you a band geek, or a jock?" Because apparently we can't be everything in a single, fabulous package? I call bluff.

I grew up knowing I was outgoing, confident, and self-assured. While I am undoubtedly all of those things, they are not the ONLY side of me. At one time, to feel like I wasn't embodying all of those traits felt like a betrayal of character. Internally, I sometimes felt sad, and scared, and REALLY unsure about EVERYTHING. Rather than looking externally for the attention I craved that could never be satisfied, I could have been looking internally for what was already there.

But I was SO SCARED to look. I was TERRIFIED that the identity I created for myself might not be who I really was. Rather than face my shadow self, I dated. I dated different ages, different lifestyle choices, different goals, and different cities. I dated a series of guys who had not a single thing in common with each other. Some guys had not a single thing in common with me. But I didn't want to be alone. To be alone meant to be with myself, and that very idea made my skin crawl.

I also didn't want to be *single.* In modern day society, it seemed to me that no greater ailment could exist for a woman between the ages of 18-118 than being "single." That seemingly innocent title carried a heavy doubt and whispered to my soul that being single must mean being unlovable and unworthy. There are many names for single women: spinster, prig, old maid. Their male counterparts, regardless of their years, have much more favorable titles: silver fox, eligible bachelor, or "keeping his options open."

Needless to say, I was socialized that to be single was the equivalent of being unlovable. So I dated guys who were all wrong, but at least I wasn't alone. If I wasn't alone, I didn't need to sit and wonder WHY I didn't want to be alone.

This was not something I was aware of at the time or even thought about intentionally. Actually, I fell in love with many of these guys. I didn't know I was hiding until I showed myself to me.

I made a lot of mistakes in those relationships, and I am not done making mistakes. The second I think I am done is when I have really failed, because it means I have slipped into a place of ego that has visions of grandeur about its own perfection. I am a beautiful work in progress and I hope that I have many more lessons to learn. From those experiences will come a deeper understanding, acceptance, and love for self. No matter the questions life throws at me, the answer is always more self-love.

All your relationships are mere reflections of the way you are showing up for yourself. The way you interact with co-workers speaks to a blockage or a blossoming internally. The kind of job you feel you are ready for, and the way you show up for the planet and its people are all interconnected. You may be programmed to believe there is one love that is PARAMOUNT above all others, and this love is a romantic love shared with another person.

But before you give yourself completely to another, share yourself *completely* with yourself.

Real Talk Questions:

What are the words you long to hear? Write them down.

_____

_____

_____

_____

_____

_____

_____

Are you waiting to hear these things from a lover, friend, or family member? Why?

_____

_____

_____

_____

_____

_____

Do you believe these sentiments are less valuable when they come from you?

_____

_____

_____

_____

_____

Where else do you sell yourself short in life and under-value your own opinion?

_____

_____

_____

_____

_____

You KNOW exactly the sentiments your heart desires. Buy a pretty piece of stationary or a fancy card and write yourself a love note.

What are some nice things you can do for yourself when you need some extra love?

_____

_____

_____

_____

_____

_____

Now go buy yourself some flowers or a bar of chocolate. You are adored!

There are over 267 ways to say "love" in Sanskrit. Two hundred and sixty seven words which depict specific ways the joy of this emotion fills up our life. Do we place a limit on our love by having just a single word in English to express the vastness of choosing to crack our hearts wide open, unrestricted and unafraid?

Please don't let the limitations of the English language place restrictions on the many ways you can fall deeper in love with self.

How can you begin to undo all the internal aches to fully embrace love? Be willing to give up who you think you should be to make room for who you truly are. All the identities you create to make yourself more loveable, admired, or respected won't mean a thing when you are alone in a room battling your internal demons. The masks you think you need to wear at work, with your family, or in relationships are simply not doing you (or the world) any justice. There is darkness in you, yes. But there is also so much incredible light. When you dim parts of yourself, you dim the whole. Share yourself as honestly as you can, then learn to love that person with your whole heart.

4

The Energy of Creation

From the time I was a young woman, I dreamed of teaching yoga for a living. Initially I just wanted to share my love of yoga and movement with others, but it wasn't long before I realized what I TRULY wanted to do was create a safe space and build community. While teaching yoga was an amazing way to do that, I envisioned having a studio space where I could build a community aligned with my beliefs and values in both yoga and life. I see all of life as yoga, and the practice has always been so much more than pretty postures in pretty pants.

I opened my first yoga studio in 2015 on the North shore of Maui. I called it Afterglow...the subtly soft and sensual way I felt after an amazing yoga or movement class. When I was opening my first yoga studio, I was TERRIFIED. What if no one came? What if I was a failure? Or the bigger question: what if I was SUCCESSFUL beyond my wildest dreams... what then?

I was already practicing ShaktiRize in my living room. The practice had saved my life in more ways than one. It was my private celebration of me. In opening a yoga studio, I felt I was putting all of myself out there for the world to see. ShaktiRize had always been a very personal practice, but I decided it was worth the risk to share it, if it brought benefit and healing to even one woman.

The first few months were challenging. Although I would go on to work much harder than I did that first year, at the time teaching seven classes per week and getting up at 5:30 a.m. was a BIG stretch. I was deeply challenged, and I was deeply in love. My mission was to bring yoga back to the people of my home island. I had felt it had gotten so expensive and "trendy" which pulled some of the magic out of the practice. I wanted to build a place where people could be safe to explore different facets of themselves. I wanted to create a place where people could discover their inner joy, find a pathway to peace, and be seen for who they really are. I think many people who open their own yoga and movement studios feel a similar way.

The studio was growing quickly, and my initial fear of no one attending classes was quickly replaced with not having enough room to accommodate all the people who wanted to participate. It was a good problem to have from a business perspective, but from an energetic per-spective, I really hated turning people away at the door who had come seeking solace in the four corners of our world.

Studio Two

I started looking for a larger location but was unable to find anything in town that spoke to my soul. Many of our students were driving from nearby towns, and I thought if I could free up some space in our existing Wailuku studio, it would buy us some time. I found a location across the island in Lahaina, Hawaii and opened our second location in September 2016. The same fears were present this time around: Was my first studio's success a fluke? Would this one be different?

While I had to navigate different challenges and learn the flow of a brand new studio with a different demographic, after a few months, our second location was thriving as well. This was a dream! This was *my* dream! I had done it. I WAS DOING it. I felt grateful. I was excited and exhausted, and my heart was so happy. I was connecting with hundreds of incredible humans every day, and I was sharing my heart with each of them.

I was also teaching up to 22 classes per week and living off protein shakes and hope. Although it was challenging, I had faith that this phase was temporary, and it would all be worth it in the end.

My intention in opening the second location of Afterglow Yoga was to free up some space in our first location. While it did that temporarily, the opening of the second location also validated our business and what we were offering. Before long, both locations were at capacity.

I had been in business for two years and had two locations that were thriving. I was working hard, but I could see I was creating change in my life and the lives around me. Positive change. I felt like I was living my dharma. I felt so grateful and tapped into my intuition. I was listening.

Laying the Groundwork

Before I opened the first studio, I was teaching yoga during the day and bartending at night. While bartending gave me the freedom to teach all the yoga classes I desired, it wasn't fulfilling me and I knew I needed to make a shift.

When my boyfriend at the time (my future husband) said to me in passing that he was looking for another "guy" to join his construction crew, I jumped at the opportunity to get out of food and beverage and try something new. I worked on his crew for a year. Because I had no experience, I was often invited to complete essential yet mundane (and very messy) tasks each day. This work challenged me to my core and often had me questioning my life's purpose.

I would like to share just one moment of magic I experienced while sanding drywall in a closet, a moment that became a pivotal point in my relationship with the universe. If you have never sanded drywall on the ceiling of a closet during the summer in Hawaii, it's a must-miss. If you do this on the regular: you are amazing. I have incredible respect for you. This type of work is no joke. Go and kiss your favorite construction worker.

I was sanding the drywall of the closet ceiling, and all the particles of dried drywall mud were falling into my face, eyes, arms and chest...basically everywhere. I was feeling *so* sorry for myself in a way that only my privilege will allow. I was thinking of how unfair life was, how I worked so hard to be the first person in my family to graduate from college, only to be cooped up in a closet as a manual laborer.

I felt like I was wasting my life. I knew I wanted to be in service to the masses. I wanted to align with my purpose and create change. Now, it could be argued that I was creating change in that closet at that very moment. That would be correct. But in my place of purpose, I knew if I was going to be sanding drywall in a closet, I would rather do it as a volunteer building houses for the needy, rather than beautifying an extension on some wealthy, white guy's mansion. What was I doing in this closet when I was capable of so much more?!

In the peak of my discomfort, I closed my eyes (maybe to get drywall mud out of them or maybe to convene with my higher power...the jury is still out) and became still. I tapped into a higher version of myself and made the universe a promise. If I could just become aligned with my purpose, if the universe would place me in a position of true service, I would continue on that path until I was instructed to stop. I promised if I was shown a path of purpose, I would give 100% of myself to it until I got a sign that I had fulfilled my end of this universal deal.

I looked up and whispered that promise to the closet ceiling and was hoping for some instantaneous revelation. Instead I got a face full of drywall dust. The universe has an amazing sense of humor and impeccable timing.

I worked on many jobs over the course of that year. Although I never got as dirty as that drywall day, I often felt my prayer hadn't been heard at all. I didn't understand why I was where I was.

I reached a point in my construction career when as Anaïs Nin says, "The risk to remain in the bud was greater than the risk it took to blossom." So I took the plunge. Only when I was putting in a bamboo floor and caulking seams in my brand new yoga studio did it all start to make sense. Our first studio required an insane build out which included ripping out partitions, painting, and removing laminate flooring. It was a bootstrap startup studio and we couldn't afford to hire anyone. But guess who was able to not only do the work, but also teach her friends how to support her in basic construction tasks? This woman here. The universe works in mysterious ways.

My intuition and universal support was truly with me on this journey, and to feel like I was aligned with a purpose was incredible. It felt like the wind on my back carrying me forward. I was working nonstop, but I was grateful to be in a place of purpose and honoring my drywall closet promise.

Studio Three

When we were only six months into our new Lahaina location, I felt a message in my gut that said I should open another studio. I was hesitant at best. It felt like personally I was barely keeping it all together. I was pouring everything into these two studios. On top of workshops, teacher training programs, and events, I barely had a moment for myself or my now-husband. I wanted so badly to say NO WAY to a third studio, but I had made a promise, and I had faith that this was my path. I started looking for another magical place for our third location. I told myself, "I'll LOOK, but there probably won't be anything out there right now." Maybe that's the energetic equivalent of a "double dog dare you" to the universe, because it took me all of seven days to find an amazing location in Kihei, Hawaii. A former dance studio, it was 2,000 square feet of hardwood potential with lime green walls. The floors stayed, but the wall color had to go.

We opened our third location in August 2017. Simultaneously, I had been searching for a larger location for our original studio for over a year, and I found the PERFECT space for our new home exactly 24 hours after I signed the lease for our Kihei location. The timing was off, but the space was so much more spectacular than I ever could have imagined, so we committed to the new home for our first studio one day later. That entire year was a bit of a blur. Less than a year into our second studio, we had opened our third location and moved our first studio into a larger location.

I loved all the people I was connecting with on the daily. I felt tired but alive. I was proud of myself for all I had accomplished, and I was so grateful to have a purposeful direction to my life. It is truly the best feeling in the world, no matter how much you don't sleep or eat. I watched the studios grow in size and success over the weeks and months, but it was the day-to-day interactions with our community, a community that I helped create, that filled my heart with so much joy and love. I feel so blessed to have experiences with so many amazing people. I hope that everyone has a chance to experience this sublime privilege of interacting with exceptional humans in their everyday life.

I knew I wanted to grow the brand, but more importantly, I knew I could use these businesses as a positive outlet to create lasting global, social change. We already had policies and practices in place that ensured we were giving back to the communities I loved in a variety of ways. We donated 100% of our mat rental proceeds each month to locally-run non-profit organizations, we had frequent donation-based classes and events to raise money for causes we believed in, and we offered free, discounted, and donation-based classes that ensured that everyone could practice regardless of their available funds. Our mission was to create a movement studio that was for everyone, even if they had limited flexibility or finances.

I had seen the exponential change that having three studios on the island could create. We were so much stronger together, and I knew that with more studios nationwide and globally we could spread the love at a more rapid rate. I dreamed of having an Afterglow community network that contributed to our world on multiple levels through multiple locations with thousands of conscious humans participating. I could envision yoga "retreats" where we could build a school for girls in Cambodia or help support a hospital in Nepal. These yoga trips would donate 100% of the profits to the task at hand. We would do yoga, but we would also allow people from the Western world to see how they could create dynamic change in the lives of others.

People in the Western world have traditionally been more financially abundant than other areas; however, our society has a poverty of soul and culture that needs nourishment. Primarily composed of traditional nuclear families, our country is younger than many *buildings* in other parts of the world, but I don't believe our capitalist system gives us the social sustenance we need to be as compassionate or happy as we could be. In places like Cambodia and Nepal, on the surface people appear to have very little in wealth or riches. Many families and communities lack the financial resources necessary to create change. However, they have a richness in culture and compassion that emanates warmth to all who share space with them.

In my vision, these yoga retreat/work trips would not be about "saving" anyone in another country, but rather an energetic exchange: we will help you with the financial and human resources you need to support your community, and you will help us find simple joy, light, and pleasure in being human again.

I knew the reasons I wanted to expand and had a purpose broader than myself. Through this motivation and with a small team of people, I spent the next year writing standard operating procedures for our business model and franchised the studios. I had a bit of interest right away, which felt like a universal affirmation I was on the right path. As I was deciding how to move forward with interested franchisees on the "mainland," I knew the process would be made more difficult with the many miles of ocean that would separate these prospects from one of our current brick and mortar locations. I decided the best way to support our mainland franchise expansion was to open a studio on the west coast in a place we loved.

Studio Four

I had done a brief stint in medical school in Portland, Oregon in 2009 and loved the city's combination of progressive and punk rock. Although the city had changed a bit since I had lived there 10 years before, the progressive environment felt like the perfect place to open our west coast flagship for future franchisees to train before they opened their own locations. I spent parts of 2018 and 2019 making trips to the Pacific Northwest with my husband and searching for the perfect place for our expansion. I found it in August of 2019 and committed to opening our Portland location in early spring of 2020. We opened in February 2020 and had 4 glorious weeks of classes and community at our new studio home.

Then the unimaginable changed everything, and a global pandemic forced us to "temporarily" shut the doors on March 16, 2020. We never opened that location again. We never opened three of those locations again.

These studios were and have always been so much more than businesses for me. These locations are my homes, and the people who attend classes and teach at our studios are my family. To lose them in one fell swoop was like losing multiple family members in a tragic instant. To say I was heartbroken is a gross understatement.

Months later, when the landlords at one of my locations attempted to take me to court for not fulfilling the full terms of my lease when my business went under, I felt the weight of those losses all over again. I felt defensive towards the things I could not change. I felt like a failure due to the loss of my businesses and questioned constantly whether there was some way I could have saved them. I felt hopeless and powerless to create change in my situation.

Even as I write this, I want to immediately insert some happy, positive things to compensate for the "negative" ideas that may arise. But life isn't always sunshine and rainbows. A trip around the world would have healed my heart quickly, but by the grace of the universe I was stuck on my home island, a place I loved deeply yet desired to leave in equal measures. One again, I had to find a path to peace, within. I hiked in volcanos and to waterfalls. I cooked food I loved. I danced. I taught classes and cried my way through the savasanas with my students/sisters. I wrote this book and learned to be a bit more patient with myself.

I'm still learning.

When my businesses shut down, I was devastated. I felt like a failure. I could only see what was no longer there. I could only see that something I worked so hard to achieve, something that had taken years of my time and energy, had been decimated in weeks.

Although everything that happened was out of my control, I felt like I had failed. I spent so many agonizing moments going over every single detail of what I could have done to bring about a different outcome. I spent so much time focusing on the things I lost.

What I didn't pay much attention to was what I had accomplished. In my loss, I didn't think about how I'd taken a $15,000 loan and turned it into a financially-thriving corporation with 100 employees in a span of just five years. In that short time, I'd grown a simple dream into four locations across two states, an online class portal, and a franchisable business model that was already receiving a great deal of interest.

I wasn't thinking about the hundreds of students I had trained across the nation and the globe or the thousands of people I had the pleasure of interacting with as I built the studios. I wasn't thinking about how I became the number six fastest growing business in the state of Hawaii the first year I became eligible. I didn't think about how I was voted Maui's best yoga teacher our first year or how our community voted us Maui's best yoga studio every year after that.

When I lay out these accolades I can see what I accomplished was incredible....IS incredible. The magic of these creations doesn't disappear just because the creations no longer exist in the same form. Magic is an energy, and like any energy, it cannot be contained through a studio location, an award, or some online portal. Magic requires movement, and movement means change, and change means that things aren't always going to look the way they did before. Sometimes it means studios close, relationships end, and situations shift, but even though circumstances have changed, the magic remains.

What I've discovered over the past year is that the energy of the things we create have their own life force. Our creations, once birthed into a tangible existence, carry a momentum we cannot control or redirect. Like any of our birthings, we would love to think they belong to us and we can coax our will onto them. But the second we bring them into existence, they no longer belong to just us; they carry with them an energy of creation that belongs to the entire world.

Our businesses, our children, and our passion projects all started out as simple ideas, and we believed in them and nurtured them until they were living, breathing, and whole. But the energy it took to bring these things into fruition is not ours, and it cannot be contained. They are a force of their own, and they exponentially affect lives based on some universal algorithm that is out of our grasp and out of our control. That doesn't mean the energy dissipates when our dreams shift course. The law of conservation of energy says that energy can change from one form to another, but it cannot be created nor destroyed. Everything we create is energy in motion, and when one form of our energy shifts, it is not dying or being dismantled. It is merely moving into another reincarnation. We have no idea of the butterfly effect of our creation. The ripples of that energy extend outwards into the universe for all eternity. Everything we create lasts forever because the energy surrounding that creation lasts forever.

Real Talk Questions:

How did the events of 2020 and 2021 affect your life?

_____

_____

_____

_____

_____

_____

_____

_____

_____

_____

What were some of the unexpected joys and treasures of this time? What were some of the disappointments and heartaches?

_____

_____

_____

_____

_____

What is something you created and loved that no longer exists in the same form?

_____

_____

_____

_____

_____

How does that creation live on through the energy it birthed?

_____

_____

_____

_____

_____

Since creative energy never goes away, how can you tap into the energy to bring more positive change to your life today?

_____

_____

_____

_____

_____

_____

5

Calling in the Wild

My loves, they've been lying to us. We've been told social lies which tell us we need to be a certain color, shape, or size to experience love and prosperity. They tell us we need to make a certain amount of money or have a particular job to be successful. Social media forces us to put on a false positivity and reinforces that navigating life's challenges and heartaches makes us a failure. We have had to fold and mold ourselves to the world's expectations. Everywhere we look in magazines, television, and social media, we are made to feel unlovable and inadequate to perpetuate the status quo of capitalism, patriarchy, and white supremacy. After all, if we aren't "inadequate," we won't need to fix anything with whatever "one of a kind" product or service they are trying to sell us. If our entire democracy wasn't built on a system that favors the wealthy and white, we wouldn't need to dive into ourselves to unearth internal biases and privileges, and we certainly wouldn't need to heal from 400-plus years of systemic oppression.

Do you feel that something has been a bit off for a while, but you can't quite put your finger on the source?

It's going to take a whole lot of love to combat the current state of the world, and I know that we can do it, but we must do it together. Although the past few years have stripped us of so much, they gave many of us a blank canvas on which to paint the masterpiece of our lives and the lives of future generations. Can we be the originators of lasting, global change? I believe wholeheartedly that we can, and it needs to start with each of us. We all need to do our part or the change won't last.

Are you ready to be an active participant in creating the world you want to see? This is not some new-age philosophy where we wish blindly for world peace. This is a remembrance of the wild *warriors* we were born to be. We are strong crusaders who take a stand for the lives we want and the world we want for ourselves and our loved ones. This is about so much more than bettering yourself just to have something to do. This is about learning to love yourself more so you can create a deep-seated confidence that is necessary for the kind of worldly change you are going to create. I want you to call in your internal wild, and tap into the innate courage you possess.

Societies were created by humans. We can "dis-create" and rewrite them in any way we choose. It starts when we stop being complacent and accepting that "this is just the way it is." When we know these ways are morally wrong or DEEPLY disserving of the diversity and differences that make this world interesting and inherently one of a kind, a change is absolutely necessary.

Are You Ready?

We can see the changes we desire in THIS lifetime. It is a beautiful time to be alive; we are at the precipice of a global, social pivot! There has never been a time of so much uncertainty and change, and we are in the center of it. We have to get out of our own way and start collaborating with womxn worldwide to create the shift the world has been waiting for.

We were warriors once, and warriors we remain, but the battles are very different now. The battles happen when we demand a shift in the status quo. The battles happen when we defund a system that is no longer serving and protecting us the way it could. The battles happen when we look in the mirror or spend too much time scrolling through our Instagram feeds. We were made to feel faulty and kept so busy to keep our eyes focused on these insecurities and distractions rather than rallying together and opening our eyes to the injustices that are happening on a much larger scale.

The war on the feminine takes place when we view other women as our competition rather than our allies and even our friends. The war on the feminine wins when we desecrate our planet for the sake of profit or fail to dismantle archaic systems that oppress the most vulnerable. There is no "outside enemy" in our modern-day warfare; we are the ones who are bringing us down. The white, male leaders of the Western world have largely let us down in creating the change we need to see. So, fate lies in our hands. Patriarchy, step aside. We can take over from here.

Women have an innate ability to band together for the greater good in times of need. We are empowered to shift the story and change the paradigm on our own. Other women are not our competition...they are our inspiration and proof that even the impossible can be achieved. So let's achieve the impossible!

What is your purpose here? My yearning is for you to tap into all the ongoing magic and freedom that is your natural state of being. Take responsibility for the life you created, then empower yourself to make the necessary changes to live your life in total alignment with your heart's deepest longings.

This is a call to action for a deeper authenticity in all of your relationships. Only from that authentic place can you begin to uplift and inspire the people around you in your inner circles, your communities, and beyond. When you are in service to the greater good, you contribute to making this world a place you want to inhabit. You have a power inside you that is as vast as the universe, and you have the ability to change lives and grow the world to greatness.

YOU ARE THAT POWERFUL!

But you can't achieve your soul's purpose and create potent, powerful change if you are too busy picking yourself apart in the mirror or comparing/contrasting yourself to fellow phenomenal females around you.

We can't band together in unity if some still lack basic universal rights and are subject to a system that was designed to oppress them. Women are woven together and interconnected. Like aspen trees, we share the same universal root system of our incredible intuition. When one of us is suffering, none of us can soar as brightly. When one of us is successful, we are all winning. So let's soar!

Finding Your Magic Again

When was the last time you tapped into the sweet magic of the world? You know, your heart racing wildly, ocean breeze flowing through your hair, in the FLOW of your life, MAGIC? All the colors were more vibrant and the stars shined a little brighter. Miracles were happening around every corner and you knew for a moment (or series of moments) that you were made of stardust and were an active creatress in the life you were leading. You remembered your life was *intentional,* there were no coincidences, and there was a true purpose for your existence.

Close your eyes and think back to a time when you felt that magic in your life. Maybe it was a first kiss with a new love, when you birthed a child, or danced on a beach under the full moon in Thailand. Whatever moment arises, take some time to MARINATE in the juiciness of that experience.

What did the air smell like? How did the temperature feel on your skin? Close your eyes and take yourself back to that exact time and place in your life and experience it completely. Go ahead, I'll wait.

Now that you are back (ooh, you look flushed!), write down that memory.

_____

_____

_____

_____

_____

_____

Did it excite you? Did it bring tears to your eyes?

Now, go a step further and write down three emotions/
sensations/words that describe who you KNEW yourself
to be in that moment.

_____

_____

_____

Now read those words again.

These are the words that describe you, my queen, in all of your beautiful authenticity. This is your natural state of being.

Close your eyes again, and imagine a place where you see your soul truly free. Maybe you know this place already, or maybe you have only been there in a dream; maybe this is a place that exists in your heart alone (that means it's always yours!). Now write a description or draw a picture in this book as a reminder.

Need some help? Conjure that moment of magic you wrote about in the previous paragraph and then imagine if that feeling were a place. (This is like an interpretive dance in word form, right?) What does it look like? Are there trees, mountains, lakes, a house?

_____

_____

_____

_____

_____

_____

_____

_____

When was the last time you felt your soul was truly free and you were tapped into your wildness? A time when you felt you were not only made up of every tree, every breeze, and every person who shaped this miraculous world, but that you could simultaneously transcend its limits? Rumi explains this best when he said, "You are not a drop in the ocean. You are the entire ocean in a drop." You are limitless. You have the vastness of the universe inside of you and you were born to shine. So dance naked under the stars, howl at the full moon, and pay attention to the unexpected miracles that are transpiring at all times. Only by calling in the wildness of the world can you tap into some of that untamed magic in self, which is where all your alchemy resides.

6

Femininity and Masculinity

If you've ever wondered whether there is a balance between femininity and masculinity in our Western world, you can perform a simple search and see the blatant discrepancies in real time. When you search for synonyms of the word *feminine*, the following words come up: ladylike, tender, womanly, soft, and dainty.

Are you rolling your eyes right now? How many of your strong, female friends would you describe in *only* this way?

In contrast, when searching for synonyms of *masculine*, you not only get ten times the amount of search results, but you also get gems like: courageous, muscular, honorable, *adult*, and powerful.

If you were an alien learning about the human race based solely on these searches, you would assume that anything masculine was obviously better than anything feminine.

As divine beings, humans are a balance of energies. Society has assigned gender roles and stereotypes to follow and we adopted them as a kind of universal truth, that women *should* be feminine, and men *should* be masculine. That to be a woman is synonymous with femininity and grace, and to be a man is synonymous with masculinity and courage. We are force-fed this narrative in books, movies, and social norms, but society's "norms" haven't traditionally supported all of us. The patriarchy isn't going to overthrow itself!

In the realm of universal energies, everything contains BOTH masculine and feminine energy, and it has nothing to do with gender. Feminine energy is fluid and spontaneous. It is both the creative and intuitive sides of ourselves. Feminine energy is nurturing and introspective. Masculine energy is linear and structured. It is both the stable and logical sides of ourselves. Masculine energy is protective and projective.

Every balanced person is a combination of different characteristics and personality traits that make each person unique. Some are more nurturing than others, and some are more logical than others. These characteristics have NOTHING to do with being male or female, and yet the Western world perpetuates the idea that being a man means masculine and being a woman means feminine.

However, if we only allow men to be masculine or women to be feminine, we are receiving only a fraction of the universe's intended energetic abundance. When we deny the duality of ourselves, we limit our scope of wholeness and remove the ability to love ourselves in all of our amazing diversity. You are not "less of a woman" because you run a Fortune 500 company. You are a woman who has tapped into her masculine confidence and focus in order to lead. You are not "less of a man" because you stay at home with your children. You are a man who has tapped into your feminine unconditional love and nurturing spirit to offer emotional support. You can be deeply connected to your divine femininity while wearing cargo pants and Dr. Martens every day, and you can fully embody your masculinity while wearing a dress.

Embodying one's femininity or masculinity does not require an assigned gender role. The goal is to create a balance in yourself and your relationships. Take my husband and me.

My husband, Andreas, was born and raised in the south of Germany. He is, therefore, more prone to an unabashed European flamboyance that makes many of his American counterparts squirm. When we were first moving in together, we were delighted to find we each had a "costume box" filled with assorted wigs, fuzzy jackets, and vintage thrift finds. Each of us has been through enough festival seasons to know it is imperative to have a costume box on hand for party "emergencies," although most people might consider even our everyday attire carnivalesque.

One day while we unpacked our clothes into our new closet, I noticed that many of the pants he was unpacking were festive and slim fit. We love to find our clothes at second hand stores, so it didn't surprise me that when I looked at the labels, many of the pants he had were "women's" pants.

My husband is very confident and never takes himself too seriously, so we often (lovingly) give each other shit.

"Babe, I love your style, but do you have any pants that *aren't* women's pants?" I said with a smirk.

He looked at his pile of pants and said, "Yeah, of course. These are men's pants." He handed me a pair of gold lame' jeans.

I looked at the label, and it said, "Cinnamon Girl."

It's one of our running jokes and one of the many things I love about our relationship. He ROCKS his clothes, and his sense of fashion is what initially drew me to him. We both love to express ourselves through unique clothing and we both embrace the duality of femininity and masculinity in each of us.

We are both. I am feminine; he is masculine. I am masculine; he is feminine.

But wearing women's pants isn't even one of the ways he embodies the feminine. Masculinity and femininity have little to do with gender stereotypes and a lot to do with the characteristics we possess that bring a necessary balance and duality to our everyday life. The femininity my husband possesses can be found in his love of art and attention to detail. It shines in how patient and lighthearted he is and how he nurtures those he loves.

However, he is not a "feminine" man by Western societal stereotypes. Quite the contrary. He is a muscular, tattooed construction worker who is an amazing protector and provider for the ones he loves. These are the masculine qualities that bring balance to his necessary feminine qualities.

He is comfortable with and honors both sides of himself, which enriches his life and our relationship.

In the same measure, I have many masculine qualities that have supported me on my journey. I am direct when I communicate and love to challenge myself mentally and physically. I am a driven leader and I take initiative to accomplish my goals and desires.

I also love to dress in flowy skirts, and I cry at movies.

I'm sensitive. I'm strong.

I'm a lover. I'm a fighter.

I'm a balance between the masculine qualities of myself that help me get things done, and the feminine qualities of myself that nurture me after a long day.

All humans are a balance of the masculine and feminine, but the toxic machismo of our society says that men shouldn't cry and women shouldn't run countries. The poison of our Western patriarchy says that women shouldn't be the breadwinners and men shouldn't wear women's pants. This distortion of masculinity and femininity *especially* in our western world has created the patriarchal society we see today from which everyone suffers.

We were taught that men and women should each fulfill certain stereotypical roles, and that if we stray from these roles we will be rejected from society. This social pressure to be either hyper-masculine if you are a male or hyper-feminine if you are female strips us of the duality necessary to create balance. We can observe this in our society when we see its inhabitants walking around deeply wounded. They have embodied the role they think society wants from them, but they are denying a part of themselves and creating an internal conflict that strips away at their soul's wholeness.

The Wounded Masculine

The wounded masculine shows up as an abuse of power. It is aggressive, competitive, uncommunicative, and overpowering. We can see the wounded masculine in many of the politicians who run our country, who are pretending to be big, capable, strong leaders, but who have not been properly prepared for their roles of leadership. We see the wounded masculine in the frat boy and football clubs who gather together to reinforce the masculine in one another, when many of them are actually seeking deeper, more emotional connections with their male counterparts.

Society does not fully support male connection in this way, and many men in their masculine wounds fear this desire for emotional support from other men reflects a deeper narrative about their sexual preference, which should be totally fine and normal, but isn't in many circles.

How many of our men need a good cry and a hug?

The Wounded Feminine

The wounded feminine feels she is never enough and seeks to bring others down. She is prone to victimhood and martyrdom. We witness the wounded feminine in the way we treat our planet and the most vulnerable populations among us. We see her rear her ugly head when our corporations choose profit over people, and our systems favor certain colors of people over others. The wounded feminine is manipulative and withholding.

When we cultivate a balance of the masculine and feminine, we enhance our ability to shift society in more positive directions. Every aspect of our personal lives is enhanced when we find a balance between both, very necessary, sides of self.

Below are some actionable steps you can take to bring greater harmony to both the feminine and the masculine. If you live a Type-A corporate structured life, I recommend focusing on some of the feminine, nonlinear tasks to bring in some balance. If you are a free-floating fairy, tap into some of the masculine tasks to bring some structure and guidance. We can ALL use a little balance in our duality. Here are some simple ways you can start to create that balance:

Ways to Nurture the Feminine:

- How tender and kind have you been with yourself lately? Take five minutes and lather yourself up with some luxurious-smelling lotion.

- What could you do to nurture yourself and your body? Light a candle and take a bubble bath with your favorite libation.

- Take five minutes to meditate and focus on strengthening your intuition by *listening* to what comes up for you. Bonus: Journal it.

- Draw, paint, write, or dance. Tap into your unique creative expression of self. Even if you question your creativity...it's in there and it wants to share itself with you! Feeling stuck? Get a paint-by-numbers or candle-making kit to relieve some of the pressure of starting. You are a creative being!

- Watch a sad movie and let yourself cry! *The Notebook* or *La Vita E Bella* always work for me! Crying can be very cathartic and taps us into the sensitivities that are so necessary to nurture the feminine. You can be a strong woman AND cry. They aren't mutually exclusive.

- Hang around with fellow phenomenal females who truly support, honor, and respect you.

Ways to Support the Masculine:

- Tap into your courage and build your confidence by doing things that scare and challenge you. Try surfing, snowboarding, or kayaking. Take a weight lifting class or go on a hike that feels outside your comfort zone. Be honest with yourself and try the thing that scares you the most!

- Bring some routine to your life by setting an alarm and waking up earlier for an entire week. Maybe use the extra time to clean your house, organize your life, and check some things off your to-do list.

- Take a martial arts class. Martial arts gives you the gift of discipline and increases your confidence in your ability to protect yourself. You are your own protector.

- Think about where you could use some clear boundaries with the people in your life. Write those boundaries down and follow through by enforcing them.
- Practice assertiveness by taking the reins of your next date night or gathering with friends. Plan it all out (date, time, place), be as clear as possible on the details, and then SHOW UP!
- Hang around with men who truly support, honor, and respect you.

Three ways I will support my feminine side:

_____

_____

_____

_____

_____

_____

Three ways I will support my masculine side:

_____

_____

_____

_____

_____

_____

7

Women Historically

A few Christmases back, my dad gave me one of those mail-in DNA tests. My paternity wasn't ever in question; he just thought it would be an interesting way to research our ancestors. When I took the test, it confirmed what is apparently true by looking at me: I am a white woman of mostly Northern European descent. However, It also showed some of the things you cannot see. You can't tell by looking at me that there is a small percentage of Native American, Ashkenazi Jew, and Arabic in my lineage. My external appearance also won't show you I was born and raised in Hawaii.

It was amazing to see how my bloodline stretched across the world into places I had never been and reminded me that to be human means to embody a mixture of many different histories.

We all have the history of countries and civilizations from which our ancestors came. These may be lands we currently inhabit or places we have never been. We have familial history, which tells a story that may or may not be linked to a particular bloodline or location. Who we identify as family can look like a lot of different things. We also have a personal history of ourselves as women.

Albert Einstein said, "If you want to know the future, look at the past." He understood that history has a way of repeating itself. We live our life in all of its intricacies with the fantastical idea that the life we are living has no correlation to the past, which seems distant and irrelevant.

We tell ourselves that the world is so changed from what it was 100 years ago. We want to believe that people are different, that we have evolved as a species, and that *our* generation is the one that will create a lasting impact on the world. I hope in my heart this is true, but if we don't understand the past, we can never shift things for our future.

How much do you know about your personal history? How much do you know about the women whose DNA you share? What do you know about their traumas and their hardships, and how do those things affect your life today?

Recent research[7] suggests that trauma can be passed down from generation to generation through our DNA. The internal aches of our great great grandmothers are as much a living part of us as hereditary traits, like curly hair or a penchant for sarcasm.

The female lineage is especially interconnected. A female fetus is born with all the eggs she will ever have in her lifetime. That means that when your grandmother was pregnant with your mother, you were already an egg in your mother's ovaries. You literally were carried in your grandmother's womb for a short time, as she was carried in her grandmother's.

They can trace DNA back for up to five generations, which is around 150-200 years. History repeats itself, and change can take time. Human evolution took around six million years to develop, and our roles as women have been changing throughout that time.

Early Attitudes Toward Women

Historically, we haven't always been viewed as equal to men. Christianity credits a woman with the first sin. In Greek mythology, it was Pandora who opened the forbidden box and brought plagues and unhappiness to mankind. Early Roman law described women as children, forever inferior to men. Western traditional recordings of history have minimized or

---

7   This includes some of the findings from the Human Genome Project: https://www.psycom.net/epigenetics-trauma#:~:text=A%20growing%20body%20of%20research,passed%20down%20to%20future%20generations.

ignored the contributions of women in different fields and the effect that historical events have had on women as a whole.

The attitude toward women in the East was at first more favorable. In ancient India, for example, women were not deprived of property rights or individual freedoms when they married. In Hinduism, which evolved in India after about 500 BC, women were required to be obedient to men. They had to walk behind their husbands, they could not own property, and widows were not allowed to remarry. In both the East and the West, male children were preferred over female children.

The intentional suppression of women greatly influenced the status of women in the West. Under the common law of England, an unmarried woman could own property, make a contract, or sue and be sued. But a married woman, who was defined as being one with her husband, gave up her name and virtually all her property came under her husband's control.

During the early history of the United States, a man virtually owned his wife and children just as he did his material possessions. If a poor man chose to send his children to the poorhouse, the mother was legally defenseless to object.

In their book, *Witches, Midwives, and Nurses: A History of Women Healers*, feminist and environmentalist writers Barbara Ehrenreich and Deirdre English argued that "witches" were actually midwives targeted by their rivals: male physicians. This suppression of "witchcraft" during that time actually deprived medieval people of alternative medicine and estranged them from ancient Earth wisdom.

The systematic tactics used to suppress feminine Earth wisdom are still prevalent today. Naturopathic medicine is discredited and seen as lesser than the allopathic route. Our government still won't allow herbs to have a list of their innumerable benefits on product packaging and even essential oils have yet to receive FDA approval. Ecofeminist Carolyn Merchant has blamed patriarchal science for "the death of Nature" in her book of that title. This is the wounded feminine present in real time.

In contrast, women in tribal nations were leaders in their communities instead of placeholders. The power that women held in the community was equal to, if not greater than, their male counterparts. The innate respect for life was cultivated through an innate respect for women. Native American women were not subservient to men. They often engaged in work—such as farming and warfare—which the Europeans viewed as men's work. They had a voice in the political life of their communities, and they had control of their own bodies and sexuality. Unlike patriarchal European societies, Native Americans were often matrilineal, a system in which people belonged to their mother's clans or extended families.

However, from the time that westward expansion began, it was not only assumed but also expected that native women would become more like their European counterparts. Throughout history, suppression and control starts with a shifted narrative. Systematically, they began releasing images showing Native American women as equal parts exotic and helpless, instead of as women capable of maintaining a civilization. These images started and then perpetuated a narrative that Native American women *needed* the support, protection, and guidance of Western men. They published these crafted illustrations as a way of gaining social permission to claim the women, their bodies, and then their lands without apology.

Even today, our media and social influences continue to portray us in hypersexualized and subservient narratives to undermine us, our bodies, and our accomplishments.

Women in Media

During World War I, many of the men in the Western world had been at war. After the war, the ones who returned home returned to a population of strong, intelligent women who had managed to maintain (and even build) society on their own. The Roaring Twenties was a time of great freedom for women and had them in positions of leadership and power that had previously not existed for them.

As media was created, women created content for themselves based on what they desired. In the 1930s, media influence (largely controlled by women) encouraged women to pursue their passions and follow their hearts. The stories in women's magazines had them actively chasing their dreams and careers BEFORE they noticed a love interest, and they certainly weren't about to give up their dreams for a mate!

Flash forward 20 years later to the 1950s, and the print media (now largely controlled by men) had shifted its message. Women were being force-fed the narrative that they should desire nothing more than to be a "housewife." The media told them they shouldn't bother getting an education because it would surely go to waste once they married.

Tests performed in the 1960s showed that the scholastic achievement of girls was higher in the early grades than in high school. The major reason given was that the girls' own expectations declined because neither their families nor their teachers expected them to prepare for a future other than that of marriage and motherhood. These women were expected to be content in these duties, and anyone who desired an individual purpose for life was accused of being too "emotional" or excessive.[8]

In many societies, childbirth, the natural biological role of women, has traditionally been regarded as their major social role as well. The resulting stereotype that "a woman's place is in the home" has largely determined the ways women have been free to express themselves, the jobs they can have, and their ability to positively impact their society. Inaccessibility to birth control due to cultural norms or lack of availability continues to make it even more challenging for women to create

---

8   Women who resisted traditional social roles could be labeled as "hysterical" and many were subjected to medical interventions in this timeframe, including shock therapy and lobotomies, often encouraged by their husbands. From this article: "Our review of the literature on lobotomies in France, Switzerland and Belgium from 1935–85 reveals that the surgical procedure was alarmingly common for female patients (84% of 1,340 subjects)." Source: https://www.nature.com/articles/548523e

world change. If a woman is nourishing and caring for multiple children, they tend to be a bit busy.

In her book, *The Feminine Mystique*, Betty Friedan talks of "a hunger that food cannot fill" when these housewives were left feeling less-than-satisfactory in their lives. This "hunger" was coupled with social shaming and self-judgment that they were not content with the life that was the epitome of the riches of the status quo. Women were put into roles that gave them very little say in the decision-making capabilities of their households and the world at large. They did not make their own money, and they were not involved in political decisions. They were subtly made to feel inferior, so they could be controlled.

Things haven't changed all that much.

Today, our advertising continues to tell us who to be, how to dress, and what size bodies are acceptable for us to inhabit. Media messaging portrays women as beautiful, young, flawless maidens who are valued only for their external appearance. We are marketed to for our youth and our ability to remain youthful. We strive for it...we would do anything for it.

We learn that if we lose these qualities, we become obsolete in the world. Irrelevant. Unlovable. The archetype of a woman in her later years is rarely represented in TV, movies, and magazines, and if she is, she lacks substance and value.

Television and movies, for the most part, only further stunt our evolution. Oftentimes, women in film are underrepresented and hyper-sexualized (ESPECIALLY Black and Latina women, and what about trans women, where are they? And Black/Latina trans women??? You get the idea).

We are usually cast (when we are cast) as the love interest or object of desire. When we do have roles that show us evolving and growing, the characters that represent us often lack true strength. Not to mention, there is still the largely prevalent archetype of the bitchy female nemesis. You know the one: she's the pretty girl who initially gets the guy/job/internship that our protagonist desires. Have you seen it?

While no single source is to blame in the Western world, our media's (and society's) influence STILL perpetuates an antiquated belief system about our roles in society and the world. This is not an old or irrelevant story. It's happening everywhere we look, and it feels calculated. If we are too busy picking ourselves apart in the mirror or comparing and contrasting ourselves to some unrealistic standard of beauty, we won't have the time or energy to notice when our fundamental rights are being stripped from us.

The Patriarchy and Healing

The patriarchy has not made it easy for the women of the world, but it has made it harder for some than for others. Patriarchy and white supremacy go hand in hand. They both exploit the vulnerabilities in groups of people and seek to perpetuate systems where the people in power stay in power, and the people who have been oppressed stay oppressed.

When we talk about the history of women, our histories spider web in different directions based on where we grew up and the color of our skin. If you grew up in Chicago as a Black woman in the 1970s, you had a very different experience than a white woman growing up in the same place at the same time. If you grew up white at any time, you have had a very different experience than a woman who grew up Black at the same time.

We need to acknowledge this so we can move forward together. Just because the trauma isn't yours to hold, doesn't mean you are released from the burden. Until all of us are free, none of us are free. It is our duty to support other people who are forced to carry the load. It is our responsibility to help change it for all of us.

History repeats itself until we change it. It is up to us to change it.

Real Talk Questions:

What does your history say about you?

_____

_____

_____

_____

_____

How has your personal history affected your present?

_____

_____

_____

_____

How has your history been different than that of a white/
Black/Latinx woman?

_____

_____

_____

_____

How has your history been different than that of a trans/
hetero/LGBTQ person?

_____

_____

_____

_____

8

White Feminism, Colonialism, and Womenkind

Our patriarchal society wants us to misunderstand each other and fear our differences, because fear keeps us divided. If we are divided, we are less powerful and more easily deterred from our mission to create dynamic and lasting social change.

If something you read or hear in this next chapter feels triggering, take a big breath and forge ahead anyway. Only by embracing the icky and uncomfortable in all aspects of yourself can you truly grow. Broadening your mind and heart to new ways of being in the world will make you more compassionate to others and will invite a newfound compassion for self.

Growing up as a white woman in Hawaii has afforded me a different perspective on race, culture, and color. I share with you this perspective with the hope that it will bring more awareness to what is happening globally.

I was born and raised on the island of Maui, Hawaii in the early 80s when the number of indigenous people still outnumbered the number of white people on the islands. Hawaii is a beautiful melting pot of people and customs that predate its entrance into American history. For over 2000 years, Polynesian people have inhabited Hawaii with their own language, spiritual practices, and socio-economic structures. The indigenous culture found in these islands is steeped in ancient traditions that are still practiced to this day. Hawaii is so much more than beautiful beaches and warm weather. It was home to a civilization of Kanaka Maoli (native Hawaiians) before it ever became a tourist destination or a state, and these indigenous people had a beautifully established community long before they were colonized by white settlers.

I consider it a great privilege to have grown up here. I attended public schools that shared Hawaiian dances, music, and myths with us from a very young age. I learned a deep respect for indigenous peoples and practices that nurtured a desire to explore more of what the world has to offer.

I was also provided a rare social experience as a white woman growing up in a predominantly non-white environment. Hawaii, like many formerly indigenous countries, had a society, language, and its own unique customs. When Captain Cook arrived in 1778, the Hawaiian language was an oral language. In addition to bringing diseases and illnesses the Hawaiian people had not previously encountered, Cook and his crew also brought a forced religion that required that Hawaiians learn and speak the "Christian" language of English. The Hawaiian language was banned a couple of years before the islands were annexed by the United States in 1900, at which point Hawaii became a plantation state for sugar cane and pineapple. Hawaii has a heavy history of colonialism being forced upon a pre-existing society.

Today, even though much of the sugar cane and pineapple fields have been replaced by houses and developments, the plantation mentality remains in the form of tourism. Most of the money from tourism either doesn't stay on the island or does not benefit local residents. While many of the tourists that visit our island paradise are kind and gracious, many are not. The narrative that the island and its inhabitants NEED entitled, arrogant white people to flood the island has been perpetuated by the corporations that make money from it. Colonialism is, and remains, a profound burden on any colonized land and its people.

I was born 81 years after the annexation of Hawaii, and 22 years after Hawaii was forced to become a state. Hawaii was robbed of so much more than socio-economic independence. What has happened to Hawaii and *continues* to happen is atrocious. Many native people can no longer afford to live on their island home due to the rising costs of homes and commodities. Like every story of colonialism, the native people have been pushed off their land to accommodate white settlers.

All white people living on colonized land are colonizers, and cause added burden to the culture and livelihood of indigenous populations merely by being there. This is a weight all white people living on stolen lands must bear; our presence has caused greater hardship than benefit to the native population.

While I didn't understand the heavy history of my island home as a young child, I did feel the burden of what I represented as soon as I started school. Being one of a few white kids in my class, it was very apparent that the sins of the colonizers who came before us had left a painful wound in the hearts of many generations. The wounds run so deep. White supremacy and the patriarchy have committed genocide, physical, spiritual, and cultural non-consensual exploitation, and have taken advantage of indigenous people for generations.

For so many years, I wished I was anything but white so I could fit into social settings with greater ease. But the world always gives you exactly what you need, and I consider being raised in Hawaii as a white girl to be one of my most valuable teaching tools. It taught me courage and compassion. It taught me empathy and ignited in me a fierce desire to combat injustices everywhere, including the injustice of being white in Hawaii. It is a grave injustice to be white while living and profiting off the nation of Hawaiian people. My presence here is a privilege, and that privilege comes with a duty to support the people of Hawaii as best I can. Hawaii is a country under siege. There is a battle happening here, and yet millions come here each year for a tropical vacation.

When I share with people on the mainland that I am from Hawaii, they immediately want to talk to me about the "reverse racism" that happens here. Racism is a construct created by the powerful to manipulate, divide, and profit from common folk. Racism has a direction in the sense that there are the oppressors and the oppressed, but reverse racism in itself doesn't exist. Even though white people may be despised by many, that is racial *prejudice*, not racial oppression. It is often hard for my (mostly white) audience to understand that the treatment I faced as a school-aged child, although unkind, did not oppress me. My perception as a young child was that it was better to be darker skinned, as I believed it was looked on more favorably from a social perspective. However, I lacked the valuable insight of the discrimination native people faced *because* of their brown skin in our colonized state. I understand now that the people of Hawaii are the ones who have been oppressed. If you are white and living in Hawaii (or other colonized lands), it is your *kuleana* (responsibility) to seek out ways you can support the community, offset the burden of your inhabitization on stolen lands, and uplift humankind.

As we are seeking to uplift humankind, we must understand that humankind has diverse needs. A white, hetero female has a very different social experience than an LGBT Black or Latina woman. By recognizing there is a difference, we can learn to be more inclusive of ALL experiences and ALL narratives. We can realize the very real need to demand inclusivity and centering of Brown bodies in our government and institutions.

During the 1970s, Black feminist scholars and activists, some of whom were also LGBTQ, developed a model to broaden feminism's definition and scope. Throughout the final decades of the 20th and the first decade of the 21st centuries, women of color published many groundbreaking works which defined and further explained some of these dynamics. In doing so, they exposed the interlocking systems that define women's lives.

The theory of those systems became known as intersectionality, a term popularized by law professor Kimberle' Crenshaw. In her 1991 article "Mapping the Margins," she explained how people who are "both women and people of color" are marginalized by "discourses that are shaped to respond to one [identity] *or* the other," rather than both.

Intersectionality is the concept that understands that we are so much more than a single, identifying factor, and that those multiple factors play a role in both our privilege and bias. It is a recognition of a single person having *multiple* forms of marginalization rather than a *variety* of marginalization. These compounded oppressions result in considerable increase in suffering, struggle, and pain.

Marie Anna Jaimes Guerrero poignantly highlights the importance of intersectionality or "indigenisms" for American Indigenous women in an essay in Mohanty's book *Feminist Genealogies, Colonial Legacies, Democratic Futures*. "Any feminism that does not address land rights, sovereignty, and the state's systemic erasure of the cultural practices of native peoples," states Guerrero, "is limited in vision and exclusionary in practice."

Our world viewpoint, opinions, and personal narrative are a result of our individual experience. This includes how we were raised, where we were raised, what our physical appearance shows to the world, and who we choose to love. Although these things truly should not matter, our external world and our society interact with us differently based on these things.

If you are a white, hetero, cisgender woman like myself, your life may have been filled with some sadness and hardships. However, your life was not made *increasingly* hard due to physical appearance or relationship preference. *Even if* you grew up as a minority in your community. Even if you felt othered in your upbringing.

Take some time to educate yourself on new perspectives and experiences. You could take a diversity course and interact with people and women who have different life experiences than you. Start by reading a book about racial and ethnic diversity.

Today, we are a product of so many factors. The great divide between women of different societies and cultures is shortened by the fact that many of us are still seeking basic rights and freedom from oppression in our societies.

Religion also plays a factor, as most world religions are not female-centric and encourage women to procreate as often and quickly as possible.

Couple this with a quickness to judge or minimize women from varying belief systems or backgrounds, and we have created a perfect storm for disempowering women in today's societies.

It's a complicated juxtaposition we have created for ourselves: Our grandmothers and mothers built a bridge for daily freedoms, and yet many of us are still imprisoned by trying to live up to standards and expectations that are not our own. We have the right to vote, but our choices rarely put us on equal footing with our male counterparts; we can go to school, work, and build community, and have access to all of the world's teachings, but our society has tended to praise us as pretty creatures who catfight for the affections of a romantic partner.

We fear what we don't know or understand, and when we don't share a common understanding of something or someone, it is much harder to have empathy and compassion for their situation or personal plight.

We can do better. We *are* better. We can't stop now.

Engage in activities that pull you out of your social circle and into ones where there is a diversity of people present. Get to know women from different backgrounds. Go into the world and see how many amazing, diverse, and interesting people there are who inhabit the planet and your personal bubble. You will be amazed to discover that, with an open heart, there is so much more that connects us than divides us. The more we come together, the more we can share our struggles and our strengths. The more unified we become, the greater the change we can create.

Exercise:

- Amplify, center, and elevate BIPOC, LGBTQ, and differently-abled voices. Read books by these authors and attend their workshops. Compensate them for their time.
- Enroll in an anti-racism or diversity course. There are many resources available to deepen your journey. One I have participated in is "ReMember Institute's Heal Thyself Transformative Initiation for People Racialized as White," taught by Rev. Brig

Feltus and a team of esteemed sociologists, griots,[9] spiritual leaders, and historians. I continue to learn so much from her and her team. You can find out more info about their courses and offerings here: www.rememberinstitute.com

Here are a few things I learned from the course:

- Surround yourself with people who are different from you and be willing to make mistakes as you navigate uncharted waters. Go into these interactions with a beginner's mindset and an open heart. If you have questions, use Google first, or pay someone to educate you. Humble your heart and tread lightly. If someone lets you into their space, respect it as a sacred temple.
- If you unintentionally offend or harm a BIPOC in your actions or interactions, and they are courageous enough to let you know, your only job at that point is to acknowledge your limited perspective, apologize, and reflect on how to do better moving forward. Please do not defend your actions, or attempt to have these people who you have harmed educate you for free. They owe you nothing.

Real Talk Questions:

Are the people you interact with everyday largely reflective of the world's diversity, or do most of the humans you engage with look and act like you?

_____

_____

_____

_____

9   "A griot is a West African historian, storyteller, praise singer, poet, or musician. The griot is a repository of oral tradition and is often seen as a leader due to their position as an advisor to royal personages. As a result of the former of these two functions, they are sometimes called a bard." From https://en.wikipedia.org/wiki/Griot

What fear do you have around interacting with people who are differently-abled, LGBTQ, and/or BIPOC?

_____

_____

_____

_____

_____

As we move into a more inclusive world, so should our customs and our everyday practices. What steps can you take to learn more about your fears of the unknown? How do these fears limit you? How do they limit your job or business? How do these fears limit your world?

_____

_____

_____

_____

_____

What steps can you take to identify where your privilege could inadvertently discriminate against and exclude people in your creations and your life?

_____

_____

_____

_____

_____

_____

Remember: Being able to work on ourselves is a *great privilege*. Having the ability to even read this book is a great privilege. Most of us have had access to enough food to eat, running water, and a free education. For some reason, the fates of the universe decided we would be blessed with these incredible gifts, whereas so many other people on our planet will never receive the many things we perceive as basic human rights.

I bring this to your attention not to make you feel guilty or ashamed (although shame may come up). This is a call to action, an invitation to step outside yourself and your own individual desires. You have an opportunity to focus on your desires for the greater good and the world you want to inhabit.

We work on ourselves so we can be of greater support to the people who need us the most. The journey to nourishing self is ongoing, and we will never be fully "done." But we can't let that deter us from showing up NOW, in all of our glorious inconsistencies, to create dynamic and lasting change.

Don't go into these new situations armed only with good intentions and a smile. Your "good intentions" have the potential to be very damaging when you don't understand the deeper implications of them. You wouldn't hop into the pilot's seat of a plane without proper training, nor would you address the scientists at NASA if you knew nothing about rocket science. You are learning a brand new way of being, and it won't happen overnight. Take a breath and get some tools before you dive right in. Thank you for being willing to show up in this way.

9

What We Do to Each Other

The #metoo movement helped shine some light on the injustices and atrocities being committed against women by men in positions of power. We let the world know we would no longer be shamed or silenced into submission. But it also found us fighting amongst ourselves as we tried to control the narrative once we had the public's attention. Although the movement created an impact, it also left some women behind.

Tarana Burke, a Black woman, started the movement in 2006 to support young Black girls who were survivors of rape, abuse, and sexual violence. The movement was largely unknown at the time because she is Black and her work centered on Black women. Only when Alyssa Milano, a white woman, posted about the movement on her Twitter account did it get the traction it deserved. Arguably Milano had a greater social reach in getting the #metoo movement global recognition; however, many critics have accused the media of "whitewashing" the movement and detracting from its intended purpose. When Milano used her celebrity status and privilege to appropriate the movement to represent a predominantly white movement against sexual harassment, rape, and molestation, she was recognized for this on the cover of *Time Magazine* alongside other activists of the #metoo movement. Tarana Burke's story appeared deep inside the pages of the same magazine. A movement she had founded was being celebrated by a major magazine, using a white woman as the spokesperson.

This is not an isolated incident.

White women have a history of ignoring the challenges and needs of women of color, because white women benefit from a racist society. They create profit and accolades for themselves when they hijack and take credit for the work of Black people. Taking control of a narrative, rather than amplifying POC voices, will only perpetuate the oppression for all of us. This is especially challenging for white women to accept, as we are still seeking balance and equality from the patriarchal system, we are still receiving the advantages of the systems of white supremacy.

We can no longer steal and exploit Black and Brown voices or take credit for their thoughts and words. It's time for us to join the groups of marginalized people to amplify, center, and empower their voices to level the playing field. When we spend our time fighting each other rather than the system of patriarchal oppression, we have already lost. That's what the elite who profit from these systems want us to do. They use our social conditioning to perpetuate it.

We turn against each other slowly and systematically. It starts with criticism of physical appearance and attitudes before progressing into judgment of other females' choice of roles in society. ("She can't possibly TRULY be happy that way.") This gives way to opposing "beliefs" on rape culture and the right to choose reproductive care, which deepens the divisions between us.

There are women out there who want to be a part of the change, but social pressures from family and friends, who don't share the same belief system, stop them from taking action. These women need our support and accountability. This isn't about creating a "safe space" for white women to hide in our privilege or center ourselves. Marginalized folks have no space that is entirely safe to them. Reverend Brig from the ReMember Institute is quick to remind me, "Only the privileged get to demand safety, and no white-dominated space is ever safe for a marginalized person." And yet, we aren't at war with one another.

Our patriarchal society perpetuates competition among women because it breeds fear, self-doubt, and divisiveness that can be exploited by the elite for money and power. When we take care of our most marginalized members, our entire society benefits. Making room for a variety of narratives and perspectives expands our horizons and opens the mind to a new way of being.

However you choose to self-identify, be it as a woman, an ally, or an activist, it's important to remember that celebrating yourself is in no way intended to diminish or demean anyone else. If your celebration of self is diminishing, demeaning, or based on creating a facade for approval, you have stepped into the role of oppressor and are stealing from another group of people.

That includes groups of people we have a hard time understanding or aligning with. We will enact a much larger wave of change when we cajole rather than command. Supporting LGBTQ rights does not mean condeming hetero folks. Supporting Black and Latinx people is not a synonym for hatred of other colors of people, and being pro-women does not equate to being anti-men. All of these ideas are social constructs used to manipulate us and cause confusion.

When someone's empowerment is another's oppression, it's thievery. There are already systems in place that have perpetuated the oppression of certain groups of people more than others. We need to focus more attention on those who have been left behind by legislation, lawmaking, and social norms, and do whatever we can to dismantle the systems that continue to create divisiveness and harm.

We can start by supporting the women we interact with all the time. These are our friends, families, and co-workers. But we can't stop there! If we only uplift women who are similar to us and already in our lives, how will we learn and grow from women whose experiences are very different from our own? How will we eradicate the systems that bring us ALL down if we stay in our safe zone of comfort?

We can start here and now.

Beginners' Guide to Uplifting the Feminine in Other Women

Step 1: Don't stay silent in conversations when people talk about how another woman is "still single," or "really let herself go downhill," or "kind of a bitch."

Whether you know the woman or not, you are being complacent if you allow others to subtly or overtly invalidate another queen. Commit to reframing the conversation through engaging questions. Gently encourage a natural shift in the conversation.

Is this woman going through a hard time?

Does she want to be in a relationship?

How can we help her? Maybe she needs a workout partner or a friend.

Remember the goal is to bring awareness regardless of a reaction. You will not be able to manage another person's reaction. Bringing awareness to certain truths will sometimes mean revealing the harmful impacts of someone's thinking and behavior. Shame is an emotion that comes up when a person's inconsistencies are revealed, when they would rather keep them hidden. It is not and should not be your priority to shelter someone from shame when you're holding them accountable for their impact.

As the late and oh-so-great Ruth Bader Ginsberg said, "Fight for the things that you care about, but do it in a way that will lead others to join you." Be clear about what is true and what serves the greater good. Dispel falsehoods and discover the many ways that social change benefits everyone.

We can't achieve that goal if we come from a place of judgment or superiority. In the same way we must do our part to dismantle racism in our society, we must also dismantle misogyny and misogynoir[10] when female perpetrators are at the root. Hatred for other women is a deep

---

10 Misogynoir is misogyny directed towards black women where race and gender both play roles in bias. The term was coined by queer black feminist Moya Bailey, who created the term in 2010 to address misogyny directed toward black women in American visual and popular culture. From Wikipedia: https://en.wikipedia.org/wiki/Misogynoir

wound that needs healing. When we treat other women poorly, we are giving other people permission to do the same.

Be mindful of how you are perpetuating the belief that women don't get along with one another. Do you participate and even start the types of conversations that oppose this narrative? Many of us don't, because women are expected to be "nice" above all else. We were taught to avoid conflict and confrontation. It's ok to acknowledge that in yourself. Being honest with yourself is the first step in creating internal change. Once you recognize how you participate in these conversations, you can create a shift. We have to foster truth and social accountability without white supremacist, punitive practices.

Step 2: Ask for clarification when your romantic partner says, "You aren't like the other girls" (as if being disassociated with your fellow queens was a compliment).

Step 3: Check in to see where the following narrative comes from: "I have way more guy friends than girlfriends because girls don't really like me." Are you making yourself approachable to other women, or is this just something you say so that you don't need to make yourself vulnerable to them? How could you make more of an effort to engage women in the activities you love that are traditionally male-dominated?

Step 4: Go out with your girls JUST to have an amazing time with your women! Get all dressed up and make this night a "no hook up zone" at least once in a while. Get off your phones and enjoy one another. Take the selfie, but then LISTEN to one another. Be present.

Step 5: Broaden your horizons on what being a "woman" looks like. You live in an incredible time, and people are embracing the feminine sides of self around the world: trans women, non-binary yet female-identifying women, and men who have a feminine side they love and honor. Embracing the feminine comes with a compassionate acceptance of things you may not understand or know little about.

Embracing the wild warrior woman within means putting yourself outside your comfort zone, educating yourself on new topics, and integrating with humans who are not the same as you. If you have been viewing the world only through your own limited lens, you're missing out on the many different colors, shapes, sizes, and backgrounds of the women around you. Listen to their stories and seek connections with women who are different from you.

Ok...confession time.

Get it off your chest, into this book, and be free of it.

Ways I have forsaken the feminine in others:

_____

_____

_____

_____

_____

Ways I have forsaken the feminine in myself:

_____

_____

_____

_____

_____

These are the (new) ways I want to show up for women in my world:

_____

_____

_____

_____

_____

I will commit to interacting with and being in service to women of different shapes, colors, ages, and socio-economic backgrounds in the following ways:

_____

_____

_____

_____

_____

Let's change it all.

If we take a complacent, backseat approach, it won't change. We are building the society we want to live in, starting with a foundation of essential human rights. That is why we are removing any barriers we have as we step into our own greatness. Greatness does not diminish or make trivial the pursuits of other women.

At the core, we all seek a deeper connection with one another. We had it once, lifetimes ago, and it was so ingrained in our psyche and cells that we feel like we are coming home when we experience it this time around. We remember when we gathered in community with one another to laugh, cry, and celebrate the great pain and beautiful responsibility that comes with being a woman in the world. We reveled in our deep and innate connection with the earth, synchronized our bodies to the moon (when we let them), and came together in the oh-so-necessary "red tent" time where we could share our heartbreaks and our triumphs.

What we need now is women who have come alive! Women who are able to breathe passion into what they do, AND be supported by other women. We need a purpose greater than ourselves, and we need to refuse the roles that have been smothering us since before our birth.

The Dalai Lama says that the world will be SAVED by Western women. While we may not be able to change everyone's perception, we can definitely do our part. As Western women, we have been gifted an

AMAZING opportunity to have access to the funding and freedoms that can begin to create positive change. We can use our immense privilege to pivot the entire world.

When we learn to love and empower ourselves first, only then can we allow this love and compassion to trickle out to the masses. THIS IS IMPORTANT WORK WE ARE DOING FOR THE WORLD. Let's RIZE UP my Warrior queens! The world is ready for us!

10

Shadow Work

Shadow work is the process of becoming aware of the aspects of self we deem undesirable or unworthy of love. These are the characteristics in self that are often deemed "inadequacies" or "shortcomings." However, these perceived "flaws" can become our greatest strengths when they are channeled properly. To utilize them as the wondrous gifts they are, we must first identify what the shadow side is. According to Carl Jung, "Shadow work is the path of the heart warrior." So let's get courageous, my warrior sisters, and dive right in.

I'll go first. I have a confession to make: I am the *least* patient yoga instructor you may ever meet. I pretend to be all peace, love, and patience when the studio setting requires it, but I am more accurately, "Hurry the fuck up." I was born impatient. I have always felt there was simply not enough time to do all the things I desired to do. I blame it on being a goal-setting double Capricorn.

I tend to be patient with other people, but the patience I have for myself is minimal on a good day and non-existent when I am really beating myself up. When things don't flow as quickly as I desire them to (which is almost always...but at least I'm consistent), I am prone to feeling discouraged and frustrated. I question everything, and this makes me very fight or flighty. In those moments I tell myself, "If it's not working now, it will NEVER work, so what's the point in continuing?"

But impatience isn't my only shadow.

I'm calculating, impulsive, and sometimes prone to sadness. There's a wounded little girl inside of me whose tears may never be squelched. (That's inner child AND shadow work in one!)

I'm bossy, stubborn and willful.

I'm prone to codependency in my relationships. I'm sensitive and sometimes take everything personally.

In short, I'm a glorious juxtaposition of character traits and tendencies that make up one perfect mess of a human, and I'm so grateful I get to be her.

But no one is just one thing. Just like everyone, I have multiple other sides of myself to share.

I am passionately truthful and committed to eradicating injustices in my community and the world. I'm always striving to become a better human and seek to be in integrity in every aspect of my life. I'm a big sister to the world who is fiercely loyal and loving toward all my "siblings."

The shadow side uncovers some tendencies that can be turned into strengths. For example, my impatience has been a beautiful driver to create and manifest the world I want. I don't sit around waiting for things to come to me; I take actionable steps to make things happen. My stubbornness becomes perseverance when channeled properly. I'm a dictator when my shadow is left unattended, but when I USE IT to channel my power, I'm a badass boss babe who built five studios, an online platform, and a franchisable business model in six years.

Your shadow side should not bring you shame. You should befriend it, because you and your shadow will reside in the same human home, whether you get along or not. Kind of like a relative you cohabitate with, or your college roommate: you don't have to always see eye-to-eye on everything, but life is much more pleasant when you coexist...and maybe even co-create. Get down into the nitty gritty with yourself and see what's there.

Your shadow side focuses on one part of yourself, so please don't beat yourself up over it. Your shadow side has even less influence over you once you learn to love and accept your glorious inconsistencies and limitations. These "shadows" only fall into a negative light when they're distorted due to avoidance.

After being mindful of my shadow side, I am (maybe) slightly more patient…on a good day. But I KNOW I am inpatient, and in that knowing, I have given myself an opportunity to cultivate new tools to support me being me in my life. On my path to patience, some of the tools that work for me are to meditate every day before I get on my phone, exercise to relieve the stress of a timeline, and (most importantly) choose which situations (and people) are going to bring increased ease and comfort into my life. It took me a little longer than others to embark on a journey of self love. I didn't recognize that all of my "ugly" and "shameful" sides also deserved recognition and a home inside me.

Conditional Love

When we ignore our shadow side, we create a conditional relationship with ourselves. This brews into a conditional love that believes we are only worthy of love when we show up in a certain way. It's no surprise when we attract relationships that love us as conditionally as we love ourselves. We are all reflections of one another, and our most intimate relationships are that much closer to our internal conflicts and comforts.

The shadow side of self is as much a part of us as the sunshine side. We are so often praised for our smiles and celebration, but these things show only a single side of the story. Not every emotion is happy, and not all tears are because of grief. By denying and resisting the sides of self, we ask the soul to split itself so it can exist. These sides of self will show up when we are the most vulnerable and challenged. Even when we are aware of them, they will continue to rear their cloudy cloaks, and that's okay. Creating change in ourselves is a full-time job, and the sneakiest, most stubborn character traits are the ones that require the most attention. This is not a "one and done" situation, where we work on our shadow side once and then it's forever gone. I wish!

Your shadow side is nothing to apologize for; in fact, the sooner you embrace it, the less power your shadows will have over you. There are sides of yourself you may not like, but you cannot resist any of these sides away. Swallowing these sides whole and hoping your heart can digest the heavy burden will eventually eat you from the inside out and create greater grievances in the future.

Your shadows and demons deserve some acknowledgement too; like the monster who lived under your bed or in your closet when you were a kid, you will find that shining some light on those fears will prove they aren't as terrifying as you might have once believed. Only by shedding light on a situation does the shadow become less dark and shrouded in discomfort. So get raw and real with yourself. Shadow work is uncomfortable. Your ego does not want to admit that negative feelings or destructive desires exist beneath the surface.

Society demands that we paint a picture-perfect story of our existence, and anything less is a perceived failure. Women especially are held to an unrealistic standard, and we perpetuate toxic positivity rather than raw realness.

There is no "perfect time" to do shadow work, as the work never really stops. By doing this work often, you are in training for real life. At a moment's notice, you can be ready for what the world throws at you. When you are confronted with your shadows in real time, through your interpersonal relationships or daily life triggers, you want your tools to be sharpened and prepared. Then you can be responsive to the lessons, rather than reactive to the triggers.

Shadow work will reveal all the things you have tried hard to hide from yourself and the world, *especially* your socially unacceptable desires, opinions, beliefs, and feelings. While navigating your shadow work, it's natural to think, "If anyone knew how I really was, I'd be a social outcast. I'd have no friends. No one would love me." That is a scary thought, but it's probably not true.

Trust the process and allow yourself to be invested in this work completely to see the magic you can receive from it. It's okay to be scared and it's normal to feel apprehensive. You will know when it's time to dive deep into the work of the shadow self if you are feeling rejected by the world or resentful of your current set of circumstances. Maybe you don't feel like yourself at the moment, or you find you are being reactive towards situations that would not have triggered you previously.

Your heart's clarity and soul's purpose know when you are searching for them, and will often reward you by showing up (sometimes in the least expected places!). So grab a journal and a bar of chocolate for emotional support. Stay present and alert throughout the process, observing your emotions and bodily sensations as you work your way through these questions:

How judged do you feel on a daily basis? Explore how much of that perceived judgment is real and how much is imagined.

_____

_____

_____

_____

_____

Think about the best and most enjoyable aspects of your life right now. What is your underlying fear in these areas and why?

_____

_____

_____

_____

_____

_____

Write about the last time you tried to manipulate a situation to your advantage and examine how you feel about that in hindsight.

_____

_____

_____

_____

_____

When was the last time you felt triggered by a comment someone made? Did you overreact? What was the trigger? Why did you react the way you did? What are the deeper fears that come up for you?

_____

_____

_____

_____

_____

Who do you envy or are jealous of currently? What do they have or represent that makes you feel this way? What emotions come up when you imagine yourself obtaining the thing you envy others having?

_____

_____

_____

_____

_____

When was the last time you procrastinated or avoided responsibility? Why do you think you did that and what were the results?

_____

_____

_____

_____

_____

When was the last time you sabotaged yourself? What do you think your deeper, underlying fear was in that scenario?

_____

_____

_____

_____

_____

What parts of yourself make you feel the most insecure? How do these insecurities hold you back? How do they cause you to lash out at other people?

_____

_____

_____

_____

_____

What life goals do you convince yourself you want but know deep down that you don't actually want them?

_____

_____

_____

_____

_____

_____

Where do you try to impose your belief systems on other people? What scares you about other people having their own belief systems in that area?

_____

_____

_____

_____

_____

_____

What was your biggest experience of loss this year?

_____

_____

_____

_____

_____

_____

_____

How can you actively be more anti-racist?

_____

_____

_____

_____

_____

How can you help nourish the less privileged in your community?

_____

_____

_____

_____

_____

Now a few Shadow Work Mad Libs...for fun!

Even though I complain, I secretly like feeling _____ (something negative) because it also makes me feel _____ (something positive).

The negative thought I like to repeat to myself is _____, and I'm hanging onto this negativity because_____.

If the darkest part of me were to speak its truth right now, it would say _____.

Don't forget about the shadow work that needs to be done in your community, your country...and our world!

11

Triumphant Tales and Sob Stories

Humans are storytellers. Since the beginning of time, we have used stories to share lineages, teach lessons, and to spread hope. We are the writers of our own stories, and we are also the editors. Sometimes the initial drafts of the stories we tell ourselves, and then share with our community, are not entirely accurate. Or they may be totally accurate, but perpetuating the narrative of the story is hurting our heart or no longer serving us. Our stories provide us with insight on how deeply (or superficially) our love for self truly is. By diving into some of these narratives, we are able to uncover gems of wisdom about where we may have started to fall out of love with ourselves or where the love affair first began.

Your Story

For any major life-changing event, both uplifting and heartbreaking, you write the story. Often your story has been practiced and repeated so many times that you have a common cadence in how you tell it. Maybe it is the story of how you met your current partner, or why you took that trip. Maybe it is the story of a less-than-idyllic childhood or the time you lost your job.

You repeat these stories to yourself over and over again and then share edited versions with others that portray you in the way you want to be seen. However, by censoring yourself to *yourself,* then sharing the edited version with the world, you unintentionally create tiny cracks in your soul. You send a message to your heart that there are parts of you that are not welcome in the world and you must hide this side of yourself at all costs. This creates an internal space that feels unsafe for your heart to grow and heal, which can leave you feeling scared and anxious *just being* with yourself.

What if you created an internal "safe room" where you could welcome all of yourself? What if you expanded that room to be the entirety of your being? How would you feel if you were able to be everything that you were at all times, unabashedly unafraid of other people's reactions or opinions? You would light up under your loving gaze and *remember* that you have something so beautiful to share with the world: you.

You, in all of your glorious inconsistencies and shortcomings.

You, in your spectacular humanness, who is both compassionate and kind, will most-assuredly continue to make so many, many mistakes...as humans do.

So check in with yourself and allow yourself to be seen by you. Write out those stories (you may need another book!) and remember these things do not define you. They are a part of what makes you magical. In the details of these moments you possess the wisdom necessary to navigate future, uncharted terrain.

Real Talk Questions:

What is a story (or stories) you have perpetuated? What value did that story have for you? For example, when someone asks you about your childhood, where you grew up, or how you met your spouse, do you have a "go-to" story that you share? How do your standard responses to these topics support a narrative that has allowed you to grow? How have they supported a narrative that limits you?

_____

_____

_____

_____

_____

_____

_____

_____

Who are YOU?

Beyond "wife," "mother," "teacher," "single person," etc., who are you at your core?

_____

_____

_____

_____

_____

_____

Write down 5-10 things you love about yourself. Physically, emotionally, mentally, and spiritually. **BE HONEST.**

_____

_____

_____

_____

_____

Write down your **shadow** side, your darkness, the parts that scare you a bit.

_____

_____

_____

_____

_____

Remember: You never need to share this with anyone, as long as you know it yourself. However, by sharing, the charge is released and you can be free of it. ALL of you is magnificent, EVEN the parts you wish were different.

So give it to me. The nitty, gritty, and ugly. The sorrowful, the shameful, and the still-aching. Don't sugarcoat it or water it down.

What has been happening on this journey of yours that's made it less than picture perfect? Which moments and situations challenged you to your core? Who are the humans that broke your heart into a thousand pieces and how did those situations alter you? Instead of minimizing this exercise, if anything, you should blow these stories out of proportion. Write your very own Shakespearean life tragedy and share your sob story.

Once upon a time...

_____

_____

_____

_____

_____

_____

_____

_____

_____

_____

_____

_____

_____

_____

_____

_____

_____

_____

_____

_____

_____

_____

_____

We create the stories we tell ourselves and others to fill a particular need. Although our stories may fill us with a sense of joy and accomplishment, they still limit us. They are riddled with false beliefs and attachments that don't serve our evolution. Oftentimes our stories have been repeated over and over again so many times that we no longer recognize them as stories, and begin to believe they are fact. While stepping into a victim role is certainly easier in the moment, that ease is short-lived and shallow.

If you are a human, you have been deeply challenged in this lifetime. If you are a woman, you have been encouraged to smother your problems with positivity. We have been SO SOCIALIZED to share only the good and the productive in our worlds. This sucks for multiple reasons.

First, we look to others for inspiration and proof that things can be done. If they aren't sharing a true reflection of the good *and* the bad, we can't gain wisdom and will be left to navigate our challenges alone. Second, we begin to compare and contrast someone else's unrealistic life to our own and become self-critical and judgmental of ourselves. This makes us feel sad and afraid we aren't living our best life, which often brews a defensiveness that inspires us to do the same type of "sharing." When we are less willing to be open and vulnerable with ourselves, the same is true with the people around us, and the vicious cycle is re-created over and over again.

I decided to ask some phenomenal females who I consider to be incredible leaders to share some of their experiences. I asked specifically for the dark, the challenging, the *UGLY* of what it meant to be living their dreams. No sugar coating, no "it all worked out because".... We have heard those stories so many times. Life was challenging and then... it got better and now I'm a superstar!

I don't buy it.

Based on my own experiences, and what these women shared with me, the awards and accolades you receive are such a small part of your journey. What happens in the moments leading up to those victories? "Success by living your dreams" stories are so prevalent and hyped-up. While I am an absolute believer in their existence (and living proof!), my story is not so one-sided. It's also filled with ugly crying on the bathroom floor.

It is time to remove the mask and lay down the armor you hide behind so you can FULLY experience the world as you were made to do! You must make this journey completely alone, but you will be surrounded by sweet angels who support you.

Now take a look at your sob story again with new eyes.

How do you think the energy of that thing lives on?

_____

_____

_____

_____

_____

How has your life been made infinitely better because this loss or hardship transpired?

_____

_____

_____

_____

_____

This isn't about forcing toxic positivity or "happily ever after" platitudes on your life's deepest wounds. This is about diving a little deeper into that narrative, connecting to your soul's higher self, and acknowledging that there is a part of this exact experience that has the energy to change lives in ways you hadn't even considered. Maybe that means that you need to come back to these questions (or even this section) at a later date. Remember to be patient with yourself. I am STILL coming to terms with what my sob stories mean for my life. Some days I see the magic of it all, and some days I feel the loss of it all. This is brave and important work that you are doing. I am so proud of you.

You are the creator of your life's path, so how does this story go? Embrace change and newness. Reinventing yourself while staying in the same place requires digging deeper. It's not realistic for all of us to live out our own eat, pray, love, or Stella gets her groove back...but the fantasy of reinvention when times get tough is an alluring one. How can you transform your life, short of jet setting off to a foreign country or picking up a younger love interest?

Put yourself in a position to inspire other women, and to be inspired. Let other women inspire you and seek female relationships that ignite in you a flame of passion to be the best woman you can be. Push through the weeds of self-doubt and claim your path. This is where you create lasting and meaningful change, a place where you can lovingly lift others up and encourage accountability in your words and actions. YOU HAVE IMMENSE POWER!

Make a commitment to being purely you. You are whole. You are valued. You are amazing. You are loved!

12

Having Faith

People must find their faith in the midst of fear and heartbreak, but is there a more direct pathway to faith? Some people find faith through religion. They surrender their sorrowful situation to a higher power and have faith that only the strength of this power can lead them through the darkest times.

I am a spiritual person, and I believe in a higher power. I am also impatient with myself and crave an instantaneous pathway that is not always aligned with the timeline of the divine. Having faith in the absence of proof will be one of my many life lessons.

My dear friend Amanda went missing in the Maui forest in May 2019, and it became such a gift for me. I don't mean I was happy she disappeared. Quite the contrary. What I mean is that it presented me with an opportunity to move from a place of deep fear into one of deep faith.

One day she went for a hike and didn't come home. The day her boyfriend realized she was missing, he called to ask me if I knew where she was. When I got the call, I was already in tears, feeling stressed and discouraged about the expansion of my studios. Building the yoga studio empire had been a longtime dream of mine, but now that I was in the nitty gritty of it, I was scared I was missing "the point." I was spending all my time and energy growing my business, and I worried the truth of life would pass me by. I was afraid I would only discover universal truth years later when I was an old woman, when it would be too late.

I thought about this many times over the next 17 days as we searched for Amanda in the rugged terrain of eucalyptus leaves and river canyons, unsure of what we would find. I thought about how challenged I was in my current life situation, but also how pointless that challenge seemed in comparison to my friend's current challenge. If she was alive, she was alone in the wilderness without food or water. If she had passed, she would no longer have an opportunity to share herself with the world. In comparison, my business challenges seemed trivial and insignificant.

Amanda was missing for 17 days, and I spent each of those days feeling hopeful and fearful at the same time. Hopeful she would be found, fearful she wouldn't. Terrified she would be found dead, hopeful she was already at peace.

These fears extended into my own life. Fear and hope; hope and fear. Hopeful I was making a difference in the world, that the world would be better because I was here, and terrified that none of it mattered. Terrified there was no way that Amanda could survive so long in a forest by herself, and hopeful that I was witnessing a miracle in real time. Some days, I lost my faith completely. Other days, as our island and the world rallied to support my friend, I had never felt so hopeful.

On the 17th day after she disappeared, I received a text message saying that not only had she been found, but that she was alive. I knew at that moment I had witnessed a major miracle. The days following her return were a whirlwind of emotion and media frenzy, but for me they were also a time of major self-reflection. I realized while she was missing that I had lost my faith.

There was no part of me that could comprehend she would not only be found, but would also be fine. My rational mind had overpowered my intuitive soul. The entire time we were searching for her, my intuition told me she was alive and knew we were looking for her, but my mind told me it was impossible.

I felt equal parts relief and guilt when she was found. Relief because my friend was found, and guilt because I did not think it was possible.

I had lost faith in the ability of the world to birth miracles, and I was gifted a sweet and loving reminder that miracles happen every day from that place of faith.

The Sanskrit word for faith is Sraddha or Shraddha. This simple word means something so much more than the limits of the English language can convey. Sraddha is trusting that we are in the right place at the right time. It is having a deep trust for self that builds an internal strength that is paramount on the journey to loving ourselves a bit more.

When my friend Amanda was found, I got a tattoo of the word Sraddha on my wrist so I would remember to stay faithful in the most challenging of circumstances. Even though I have it tattooed on my wrist as a reminder, I still have trouble trusting in faith. Faith feels like an unreliable and inconsistent friend at times, because I want her to adhere to my timeline. I want the magic to happen NOW. I don't want to wait, especially when my heart is hurting. But when I release her from such strict, linear (and human) ideologies, she is free to perform the miracles she was made for and I am gifted a deeper sense of trust in the ways of the world.

It is easy to trust in the ways of the world when everything is going the way we desire. It is easy to have faith when we have a job we love, a secure home, and loved ones who support us. It is so much more challenging to maintain our faith when nothing is flowing. Our most difficult moments are our *true* test of faith. How do we keep the faith when there's no food in the fridge or money in the bank account, and it feels like the entire world has forsaken us?

When we experience change and uncertainty, it is easy to wander into areas that are fear- and scarcity-based. The mind devises a thousand scenarios on our imminent demise, none of which are necessarily based in reality.

If life feels like a mess right now, it's simply because our fears are just a little stronger than our faith. Having faith asks us to trust ourselves and the ways of the world without any proof of a desired outcome. Many of the world's wisdom teachers have reminded us to overcome fear by having faith, faith in the things we thought were impossible, faith in the wondrous ways of the universe, and faith in the unimaginable and the magical.

When you trust in your life's process, you develop more courage for the future. Cultivating and keeping this courage is essential to being human. This life won't necessarily get any easier, but if you have the tools of faith and courage with you along the path, you can more gracefully navigate all the obstacles.

Having faith in these situations requires a deep courage and strength to trust that the best possible outcome is being designed by the universe for you. Every obstacle is designed so you can navigate how to overcome it, and every mistake you make is brewing the individual blend of magic your life craves. When you begin to trust those universal truths, you can release your fear and anxiety and begin to work from your highest potential. The side of yourself that operates from a place of scarcity and apathy is you in a fight or flight state that can't create the shifts the world needs. Showing up in your life from a place of fear is not going to get the magic moving.

Real Talk Questions:

In what area of your life do you consistently lack faith?

_____

_____

_____

How much faith do you have when it comes to love? Time? And money?

_____

_____

_____

Do you believe in miracles? Where have they manifested themselves in your life? How did you feel when they happened?

_____

_____

_____

_____

_____

You live in a world of ample abundance, but when your faith is wavering, it's nearly impossible to see the bounty that exists all around you. Fear takes over and faith comes crashing down. Replacing fear with faith becomes so much easier if you put your faith in something real. Meditation can lift some of the cobwebs of your mental limitations to make room for the clarity that resides within.

Read the following abundance meditation all the way through before you try it. You don't need to memorize this passage to reap its benefits. The idea here is to create an abundant space for self you can always return to when your faith is tested or you slip into a scarcity mentality.

Abundance Meditation

Close your eyes and take a few deep breaths in and out. With each breath in, draw abundance to self, and with each breath out release feelings of fear and scarcity.

Now visualize yourself on a vast stretch of beach. The white sand extends in either direction as far as the eye can see, and the ocean is a sparkling blue. Sit on the soft sand and hear the ocean waves gently lapping the shore. An overwhelming sense of peace and love inhabits your heart in this sweet space. You feel protected, safe, and secure. You are reminded that you are as expansive as the universe and that all your needs are met. You feel nourished and happy as the sun gently kisses your skin. Now see your heart's desire on that beach. Look at it from every angle and allow yourself to be overcome with the joy of being so close to what you want. Stay here as long as you like and observe the emotions that arise.

You look beautiful!

How do you feel?

_____

_____

_____

_____

_____

Do you feel worthy of this abundance?

_____

_____

_____

_____

_____

Do you trust that it is available to you? If not, what is blocking you from receiving this abundance?

_____

_____

_____

_____

_____

_____

What do you desire from this life?

Money? Fame? A new house? Write it down.

_____

_____

_____

_____

_____

_____

_____

Now take that desire a bit deeper and strip back the superficial to come to the *root* of what you want. If you said fame, maybe your deepest desire is to be loved. If you said you wanted a new home, maybe your deepest desire is to have a safe space to build community. Our superficial desires, like a new car or trip around the world, come from deeper desires. Allow yourself to get deep and honest with yourself.

What is your deepest desire in this life?

_____

_____

_____

_____

_____

_____

_____

You have shared your desire with yourself, and now it can begin to take shape. The world hears you, and these desires are making their way into your world.

How can you utilize your one, wild, sweet life to bring more faith and abundance to others?

_____

_____

_____

_____

_____

_____

_____

In my life, I have experienced a few life-altering moments when fear and anxiety threatened to consume me. It was debilitating and paralyzing...and eye-opening. I realized that love is by far the stronger emotion. Despite what news and social media will have us believe, there is love, hope, and faith all around us.

Miracles happen every day...you are one of them! Look around, see the blessings that surround you, and do whatever it takes to find and share love with the entire world.

13

Channeling Your Power

In our society, we measure power based on money, beauty, and fame. Many associate their self-worth with their abundance (or scarcity) in these three things. We struggle with self-judgments on where we should be in our jobs, relationships, and personal life. We slip into jealousy and fear around other women who shine brightly and threaten our sense of self in any way.

We make "happiness ultimatums" with ourselves and promise that "If I only had _____, I would be happy/loved/successful." Many times, we equate our value and power with how well we serve and care for others, making ourselves inadequate and unfulfilled before we even begin. We ask ourselves if we are "enough." Pretty enough. Smart enough. Rich enough. Enough!

Powerful people are the ones who are the most connected to their *internal* resources. TRUE power is carefully cultivated from within and stems from connection to self. It has nothing to do with money, fame, or fitting into a certain dress size .

Let's strip down some of our beliefs around power.

Real Talk Questions:

What is power?

_____

_____

_____

_____

_____

_____

How would you feel powerful?

_____

_____

_____

_____

_____

Write down some powerful women you admire and why.

_____

_____

_____

_____

_____

_____

These are the hidden gems that show you the woman you would like to be. Follow their lead!

Now that you are clear on who you are and what makes you powerful, you can begin to align yourself with your values and refine and deepen your essence of self to attract the life you desire.

One of the greatest gifts you have as a woman is your strong intuition. This intuition is your magical power and gives you a head start in attracting your golden life. Your intuition is proof that there is more to life than what can be weighed or measured in a lab. Science cannot explain intuition, but it clearly exists, based on your own experiences.

When you start something new in our life, such as a job, a relationship, or planning a trip around the world, you are planting a seed of faith, hope, and mystery. There is a certain amount of risk and uncertainty in any change, which is why you need to trust yourself. You can tap into the innate wisdom of your intuition and make decisions that will create the best outcome for you on your journey.

Your intuition is like a super power for your life and gives you cues as you align with who you truly are. It helps you refine the way you navigate your soul's purpose. You can deepen this intuitive side and increase greater trust in self through intentional mornings, grounding, and meditation. The mind is chattering constantly throughout the day, and it can be challenging to sort through the mindless chatter to find the gems that are buried deep within you. When you meditate, it's as if you're clearing the cobwebs of your mind so the true sparkle of your intuitive brilliance can emerge.

Running Toward the Roar

I am NOT a morning person. I was born a night owl, and all of those years of late night bartending certainly didn't help to support an early morning routine. When I was navigating the loss of my yoga studios, I struggled to get out of bed in the morning. I really didn't feel like I could face the day, and I *really* didn't want to face any other humans. It was so hard for me to process my own emotions around this loss, much less try to share them with others. I was a changed person, but I wasn't sure how to convey that in words to the people I loved. I often found myself alone. Even though I craved people and support, I self-isolated rather than show myself to the world in that state.

There is an old African proverb that teaches us about fear. The teaching shares the hunting practices of lions. The oldest and weakest lions, though they have lost all their teeth and can no longer hunt, have a ferocious roar. The pride of lions positions itself on a path in such a way that the oldest lion waits on one side, whereas the younger, more agile lionesses, who should be feared, wait on the other side of the path. As the potential prey walks along the path, the oldest lion lets out a savage roar with the intention of scaring the victims into the grasp of the younger, more ferocious lions. Only by running *toward* the roar can the pursued find freedom. In the same way, our salvation lies in taking a leap of faith and running *toward* the roar.

While talking with a friend of mine about my predicament, she shared that she had started something called the 5 a.m. club, where she would wake up at 5 a.m. to meditate and journal before the rest of the world woke up. As a proven non-morning person, 5 a.m. was the middle of the night for me. To wake up at that time legitimately scared me, but I decided to give it a shot and run toward the roar.

While waking at 5 a.m. may not feel like the equivalent of being devoured by lions, it was a big stretch for me. Waking up at that time changed the entire world for me, and it definitely changed my perspective. Those morning hours were filled with beach walks and quiet cups of tea. It gave a kick start to showing up for myself and the world in a different way because the world felt so different. In those early morning hours, while the rest of the world slept, I rediscovered my power. It had been there all along, but my loss had transformed me, and it had transformed my power. It was stronger, more potent, and in a different place than I remembered. Only by turning off the external noise and mindless mind chatter was I able to discover the new pathway to my strength and my salvation.

Mastering the Morning

Although my mornings typically start closer to 8:00 a.m. now, I retained some of the magic from my 5 a.m. experiment. A typical morning for me starts with 20-30 minutes of meditation as I find the rest of my day flows MUCH more smoothly when I do. The length of time I spend meditating doesn't seem to matter as much as the consistency. On the days I meditate, I am more grounded and aligned with my intuition. I also found that (no surprise here) meditating BEFORE I scan through my phone greatly improves my day.

A meditation practice can be an incredible tool to discover your authenticity. You can clear the cobwebs and clutter of the mind and open a gateway deep inside yourself to discover the magic within. It is a direct link to your source of personal power. How could your world shift by shifting your routine?

Real Talk Exercise:

My *ideal* day starts with....

_____

_____

_____

_____

_____

_____

_____

_____

_____

Write out a *feasible* morning routine:

_____

_____

_____

_____

_____

_____

_____

BONUS: Stick to it!

Begin a meditation practice. Start with five minutes a day and see where it goes. Journal what comes up for you and welcome any and all insights to your internal landscape.

Not sure where to start or feel a bit discouraged? Try some sunshine play. This is my go-to tool when I am feeling discouraged and burnt out. I wanted to create a practice that was the opposite of Shadow Work, so Sunshine Play was born.

Sunshine ✴ Play

You will always have problems and obstacles to overcome. These things are *never* going away, but it doesn't mean you need to constantly focus on them. Sometimes it's nice to take a step back and remember why this life is sweet and worth living. I call this exploration "Sunshine Play" because even though it's "work," it shouldn't feel like it takes much effort. As you are discovering your ideal morning routine, make time to let the sunshine in, within. Feel free to go through some of these exercises and journal prompts when you need a little extra light(ness) in your life. xoxo

Make a gratitude list.

_____

_____

_____

_____

_____

What would you do if you knew you could not fail?

_____

_____

_____

_____

Write a positive advice letter from your future self or write yourself a thank you letter...then mail it to yourself!

_____

_____

_____

_____

What ten things make you the happiest?

_____

_____

_____

_____

_____

What do you need more of in your life right now?

_____

_____

_____

_____

_____

Beginnings matter. The way you start a new job, experience, or relationship will set the tone for the moments that follow. Just like you wouldn't show up late to a job interview, you also want to respect and honor your time. In your relationship with self, it is even more important that you start your day intentionally, filled with love, if you desire to see love reflected back to you.

Morning routines matter, and they can change your entire world. These morning routines don't need to start at 5 a.m. with 100 sun salutations and meditation practices that last for hours...but they could! The most important thing is that your morning *works* for you and sets the tone for the rest of the day (and life!) you want to have. Be patient with yourself, and remember that embarking on any sort of new journey can be a bit intimidating, but know that this time you spend with yourself is golden for your life's purpose.

Here are some of my favorite meditation techniques for intuition and manifestation that can be done in five minutes or less. Combine them for a longer practice, or use them as your go-to tools to clear away the stressors and the cobwebs:

Grounding Cord Meditation

Sit comfortably or lie down. Gently close your eyes and take three big breaths to center yourself. If you have more time, and you feel called to, you can spend a few moments just focusing on your breath. When you feel ready, visualize a grounding cord starting at the very base of your spine. This cord is a rope of light that begins to extend downwards from your spine. Your grounding cord extends beneath the surface you are on. It extends beneath the building you are in, and anchors 20 feet into the earth beneath you. You are safe here; you are nurtured. Feel Earth's energy flowing up into you through your grounding cord, and deposit any energy that feels too heavy for you to hold into the earth beneath you. Continue this energetic exchange for as long as you need. You allow all of your sadness, frustration, and uncertainty to travel down your grounding cord where it is absolved into Earth's loving embrace. Earth energy travels up your grounding cord and provides support, wisdom, and strength. Continue to breathe the entire time. If it feels right, you can inhale as you receive Earth's recharging and exhale as you leave behind everything that is not serving you. When you feel complete, gently remove the grounding cord from 20 feet beneath you, and feel the cooling energy of the Earth as the grounding cord retracts back into your spine. Notice any physical sensations accompanied with drawing your grounding cord back into your body. Do you feel a little lighter? Repeat this meditation whenever you need a little grounding and support.

The Movie in Your Mind

You are probably thinking, "But I'm already in my mind so much. Why would I want to spend more time there?" I get it, but this is different. Find a comfortable seat or extended position and close your eyes. Take a few deep breaths to ground yourself. Now with your eyes closed, begin to stare at the backs of your eyelids. It sounds a bit, um, impossible to do, but once you give it a shot, you will notice that behind your eyelids is a dark screen, similar to a movie screen. As you stare at this empty screen, you may begin to see shapes and colors appear. Watch those colors and shapes shift and change on the movie screen in your mind's eye. Maybe those shapes become images, or faces, or short films. Maybe these colors actually transform into a full length feature! Be open to what you might "see." Allow the images to float onto the screen without an attachment to any outcome. Similar to watching the clouds pass by on a sunny day, observe a shape, let it morph into another shape, and then let it pass by. Let your mind wander in and out of focus and stay in your own home theater as long as you like. Have fun! When you feel ready to return to the world, simply open your eyes. You are welcome to journal any insights you received from your personal movie, but take it all with a grain of salt. Sometimes the mind simply needs to download superfluous images to create more space for the important stuff.

Defining Your Bubble

This is one of my favorite techniques and it's super simple to do. Find a comfortable position either seated or lying down. Flutter your eyes closed and begin to bring some deep, mindful breaths into your body. Now visualize a giant bubble. The bubble envelops your body completely. It goes above your head and under your feet. There are no rips, holes, or tears in this bubble, and you are completely encased in its safe circumference. Now as you sit in the center of your bubble, entirely enclosed, it begins to fill up with a colored mist. This mist is your favorite color, and it completely surrounds you as you reside inside the bubble. Enjoy the sensation of this colored mist on your skin as you begin to focus on your breath. As you inhale, you inhale a bit of the colored mist into your body, where it permeates every cell and inch of your being. On your exhalation, expel any colors inside you that are not this color. The browns, the blacks, and the greys all travel from your body and pass easily to the outside of the bubble. You breathe in again and take more of that nourishing, colored mist into your being. On your exhalation, all the other colors release from you and go to the outside of the bubble. One more BIG, deep breath as you inhale ALL of the colored mist inside the bubble. HOLD it in for just a moment and feel it electrifying all your tissues. Notice how you sparkle up! Then on your giant exhalation, the bubble that encases you gently pops off your body and begins to float skyward. The bubble floats higher and higher and higher with all of your sadness and sorrows, all of your aches and pains. It travels up, up, up into the sky until you can no longer see it. Stay here for a few moments and notice how you are exceptionally energized and restored from the colored mist. May the rest of your day be filled with gems that are worthy of your shine.

Please remember, not every technique works for every person. Try them all out and use the ones you love for now. Don't force yourself to meditate in a way that doesn't flow for you. Come back to each of the different techniques periodically. You may find that even though one "didn't work" at one point in your life, it is now your new favorite. Also, look into a meditation app. There are so many great ones available now that allow you to explore what you like best.

Here are some meditation apps I love:

- INSIGHT TIMER
- Chopra
- Also YOUTUBE has a ton of amazing (free) content.

14

Move that Body

I t is a true GIFT to explore ways to enhance your power so you can better yourself and our sweet world. While meditation will help you tap into the deepest parts of your internal self, you are still a physical being who moves about this realm in a physical form. You can't just focus on one aspect of yourself if you want to discover the most authentic and complete woman you can be.

Yoga philosophy sees the body as a vehicle for the soul on its journey towards enlightenment and discusses not one body, but three. First is the physical body which is born, grows, and changes. Next is the astral body which contains your emotional and spiritual self. Lastly is the seed body, which contains the blueprints for who you are and who you will be from lifetime to lifetime. The physical, spiritual/emotional, and seed bodies make up crucial components of you. Connecting to the internal and the spiritual sides of self are a part of diving into the depths of you. But, you also need to move your body!

One of the biggest problems in our Western world is that most of us are so *out* of our bodies. Many sit at desks all day, in front of computers. We grab meals that are "convenient," but not very healthy or nutritious. If we do manage to fit exercise into our daily hustle, the movements are often directed and linear, like riding on a stationary bike or running on a treadmill.

Although any movement is beneficial for the body, we rarely tap into how we *feel* in our body while it is moving. More often than not, we try to change and manipulate the body to take on a new shape or external appearance. Our bodies are rarely celebrated in all of their beautiful uniqueness and inconsistencies. The powers that dictate societal standards through marketing and media want us to be disconnected from these bodies, making us an easier target for the $71 billion dollar weight loss industry.[11]

Did you somehow learn there was something "wrong" with your body? When did it happen? As a baby, you had no concept of your shape or size. Babies are not insecure or unsure about their bodies until they are taught they should be. Your body's shape and size was most likely determined before you realized it may not measure up to society's standards. But when you were a baby, you didn't know that society wanted you to care. Whenever you saw a mirror, you ran up to it and kissed it with a slobbery, open mouth because you were so excited to see your physical form reflected back at you. I bet you haven't done that in a while. Your body, like mine, can be subjected to all forms of weight loss and exercise routines. You can starve yourself and work out for hours each day (many of us have), but your true shape and size will always be screaming to be released from these self-imposed shackles. Your true physical form is craving your love, nourishment, and acceptance exactly as it is. Can you show yourself that love at any shape and size?

I know what it means to have a non-comforming body. I was born curvy. My body possessed an ampleness from birth that seeped outside the lines of society's comfort. There is a picture of me at around two years old, standing in our yard with a T-shirt, underwear, and rain boots under my thick thighs. I was already muscular; I was already strong. My body type was decided long before society's standards could influence me. My

---

11 According to researchandmarkets.com. This number is a 9% decline for 2020. Previously it was $78 billion. Source: https://www.researchandmarkets.com/reports/5057591/status-report-of-the-u-s-weight-loss-market-in

thickness was as much a part of me as my straight hair or stubborn personality, things that could not be changed no matter how hard I tried. Society views my stubbornness as a shortcoming, something I should tame or control. My full hips and big breasts are equally stubborn, unwilling to pour themselves into jeans and underwire without a fight.

Both of my grandmothers are thick. They are ample-bosomed and abuntally-waisted, with biting wits, sharp tongues, and full laughs. My mother and father are both thin, which proves that thickness, like twins, is a rare gift, and may skip a generation.

In society's newfound hunger for more plus-sized bodies, I fall shy of many of the expectations and standards. Still, I love my shape and my size. It is perfect for everything I love to do and what I need to accomplish. My thick thighs allow me to go on multiple day hiking adventures, my strong arms never tire from squeezing loved ones, and my curvy hips keep the tempo as I dance until the wee hours of the morning. My favorite people are thick. Their external contours and curves hint at the complex landscape that lies beneath the surface.

My body was made to move, as was yours, yet so many of the movement modalities don't tap us deeper into *being* in our bodies. Yoga is amazing for developing the mind/body connection and can provide the awareness necessary to begin to understand the physical and emotional relationship. But dance infuses energy into all our glorious curves and amplifies it all.

Most of the world's traditions have incorporated dance in celebration and ritual. A civilization's dances, along with its music and language, are among the primary personifications of that culture. Dances tell the stories of ancestors, depict the culture's myths, and are used in religious rituals. Our ancestors knew the power of dance to connect with the spirits and our higher self. And yet, tragedy of all tragedies, most people "don't dance." They don't allow themselves to succumb to the freedom that arises through unchoreographed, non-linear body movement.

Dance has a special relationship with the feminine. Non-linear, spiraling movements help to ignite the "shakti" or divine feminine energy in all of us, an energy that could use some amplifying in the patriarchal societies of the West.

All creation begins in this life-giving energy. Some dances even support childbirth. Certain movements in belly dance prepare females for the stresses of childbirth. The Hawaiians have Ohelo hula, traditionally performed in a reclining position by both sexes, to tell procreation stories and tone reproductive organs. The Maoris of New Zealand also have childbirth preparation dances involving pelvic and abdominal muscles. Dance and body movement are essential to the cycles of life!

Only when you learn to love, admire, and respect your body, can you create a gorgeous vessel befitting of all your sweet light. Remember you are whole, beautiful, and powerful, and nothing in your past can make you broken or unredeemable. Let's write our own myths, ones that make you glow! Your myths can have the heroine (you!!!) help others to heal.

Exercise: Move Like No One Is Watching (They Won't Be)

- Turn on your favorite music and move that body.
- Notice where emotions rise.
- Dance through them.
- Don't "perform."
- Tap into your body's ancient wisdom and let it move. The body knows what it needs, so lay down those layers of resistance and let it groove!

Now answer these questions:

How do you feel about your body? How do you feel about its shape, size, and color?

_____

_____

_____

_____

How would it feel to be free of expectations for this body?

_____

_____

_____

_____

_____

How can you support a deeper love and appreciation of this body?

_____

_____

_____

_____

_____

Want more juicy, sensual body movement?
- Check out a pole fitness class in your local town.
- Take a ShaktiRize class online at www.shaktirize.com.
- Find a women's ecstatic dance event near you..and show up!

Claiming loving acceptance of your physical body, while surrounding yourself with sisters who LOVE their bodies too, is the ultimate act of self love. Through movement with other women, you can purify your vessel and cultivate a deeper relationship with the only body you have.

Self Love Exercise: The Photoshoot Project

It's just that. Take a day (or 20 minutes) to photograph yourself in a favorable light. You can go all out and get a makeup artist, hair stylist, and professional photographer to style you for your shoot, or it can be you and an iPhone on a Tuesday morning.

It doesn't need to be fancy, but it should be something that makes you feel as fun, sensual, and beautiful as you want to be.

Here are some ideas:

- Boudoir Shots (You are sensual; you are beautiful; you are worthy of seeing yourself in this light.)
- Glam Shots (Get your makeup and hair done...you are a superstar.)
- Ancestral Shoot (Do some research on your ancestral roots and tap into that for a photo shoot. Channel your great grandmothers and tap into some of their power.)

Keep in mind, you aren't doing any of this for the 'gram. If you are feeling yourself and you choose to share it...that's amazing, especially if you are an indigenous woman, a trans woman, or a differently abled woman in any way. We need more representation of all of these types of women to fill our feed on the daily. Creating normalized conversations and admiration around all of these beautifully different physical forms is what helps to propel social change, AND it contributes to more sensual self-love.

However, the main idea of your photo shoot is to have a tangible representation of yourself in a gorgeous light. Do the shoot that scares you the most! You are ravishing before the photo shoot, and you will continue to be afterwards, but photographic reminders of your magic in physical form are the gifts that keep on giving you the confidence you need to change the world.

15

Honoring Your Sensuality

In our culture, there is an unfortunate abundance of fear and distortion around the topic of sex. We are sold all kinds of products through sexualized marketing campaigns, and then we are expected to cap that same energy in the real world. We are expected to be both the virgin and the whore simultaneously.

In many ways we have suppressed our sacred, sexual juiciness because of the reflections we receive from men AND women. This is unbelievably tragic, as our sexual energy forms the deep roots of our creativity and passion. Our sexual and creative energy stem from the same place...our sacral chakra center! Your sexual energy is your creative flow, and when you channel it consciously, everything you do becomes your art. When you let yourself move in a way that is sensual without any "end goal" or expectation of another person, you tap into the sweet nectar of yourself that allows you to blossom more fully.

When you own this sexuality as your inner fire, it no longer becomes a physical act centered around your genitals but rather a tool to bring passion to **ALL** areas of your life. This means going beyond your fear of power and letting go of trying to be a non-threatening little girl or over-the-top sexpot. This means releasing the habit of putting everyone else's needs before your own. Honor your sexuality-FOR YOU! Release any fears you have around that great power.

Real Talk Questions:

What are some beliefs you have around your sexuality?

(I am a prude, I am not good in bed, If I behave a certain way I will be a "slut"...etc.)

_____

_____

_____

_____

_____

Two areas that affect sexual expression are body image and fear of power. How do you feel about your body?

_____

_____

_____

_____

_____

_____

What power do you feel from your sexuality? Is it distorted?

_____

_____

_____

_____

_____

HOMEWORK: Dance naked in front of a mirror and WATCH yourself for an entire song. But don't just watch yourself, look yourself in your own eyes and *seduce* yourself!

How did that feel? Scary? Powerful? Intimidating? Beautiful?

_____

_____

_____

_____

_____

_____

The first time I decided to try the above exercise, I was SHOCKED that I actually felt embarrassed to look myself in the eyes. This was not because I felt any shame or judgment for my physical form, but because I felt *intimidated* by the power I saw staring back at me. I had shared this part of myself with people in the past, but I had never treated myself to this compelling reflection of the supernova I truly was. I hope that it is as sweet of a revelation for you as well. You are so stunning and unique, and your physical form and sensual side are worthy of being seen and honored through a loving gaze. Let that initial loving gaze be your own. Then, should you choose to share it, welcome in the person or persons worthy of all the magic you contain.

There is a massive difference between unconsciously diluting your sexual energy by sharing it with the masses and consciously accessing the vital energy and life force that is your birthright. One is a desperate expression of need and a desire to feel loved through sexuality, and the other is a powerful claim on your right to pleasure and creation in all forms. Don't be afraid of your passions. Allow them to fill you and inspire you. They are among your greatest treasures.

Choose wisely with whom you share your passion. Many of us have been wounded by stolen or undesirable sexual experiences. Use your breath to bring love and acceptance to the places that have been hurt. Release any energy that doesn't belong to you. You can heal. Remember that your nature is to flow, and NOTHING, no past experience, event, or person can take your sexual essence away, and it can NEVER be broken.

I recommend the following resources if you need support in healing through sexual traumas or supporting others on their journey:

Rape, Abuse, and Incest National Network

RAINN is the nation's largest anti-sexual violence organization:

https://www.rainn.org/

CALL 800.656.HOPE (4673) (offers support 24/7)

The National Sexual Violence Resource Center

NSVRC provides research & tools to advocates working on the frontlines to end sexual harassment, assault, and abuse with the understanding that ending sexual violence also means ending racism, sexism, and all forms of oppression.

https://www.nsvrc.org/

16

Tapping into Your Own Magic

This chapter contains some amazing tools that I hope will help you navigate your beautiful and complex internal landscape. Go through them as you see fit, as many times as you desire. You are a constantly changing and evolving human being, and even though the rituals and meditations are the same, you won't be. They will have a newness necessary for healing and a bit of the familiarity required to create a safe space to do the work.

CHAKRA Magic

We are all channels of divine energy. Yogis believe we have a series of chakras that help regulate that energy so we don't burn out or skip into complacency. Keeping those channels cleared and open is paramount if we want to be in service to one another and the planet. You can't pour from an empty cup and you can't give from an energetically depleted system.

As humans we will make mistakes and create imbalances in our lives. Maybe we raise our voices with our kids or partners; maybe we find ourselves manipulating a situation to get an outcome from a selfish desire. The question is not whether we are going to get energetically out of balance at some point (we will). The question is, how do we restore integrity with ourselves and others to return to balance and continue on the path of world change?

One of the ways to fine tune our energies is to clear those chakra channels through movement, meditation, and journaling.

Although science does not necessarily acknowledge the existence of chakra systems, it is interesting to note that the chakras all align with organs in the endocrine system. The endocrine system governs all sorts of scientifically-accepted bodily functions like our metabolism and hormones. The endocrine system, in conjunction with the nervous system, helps to regulate and adjust the body's hormone flow to keep us in optimal health. While the endocrine system is fundamental to our well being, there is still so much about its processes and the way it regulates itself that is a mystery for many in the medical community.

An imbalance in the nervous or endocrine systems creates an imbalance in our entire body; this is true of chakra systems as well. Our chakra system allows us to conceive that a subtle energy, such as love or positive intentions, can actually change the physical body, especially through the endocrine and hormonal systems. This may seem far-fetched, but the location of the seven chakras physically aligns with the location of our endocrine glands. It's important to recognize here, that our Chakras and their energetic focus pass straight through the body. Sacral is the abdomen, AND the lower back. The throat is the front of the throat and the back of the neck. The third eye is between the brows and at the base of the skull. Let's explore each of the seven chakras in more detail.

Root Chakra—Adrenals

Our adrenals create adrenaline and the hormones that regulate blood pressure and stress. These hormones are effective in regulating stress and are essential to our "fight or flight" response. The root chakra is associated with physical survival and feeling safe.

Sacral Chakra—Reproductive System

The ovaries and testes create hormones that control an individual's sexual development and maturity. The sacral chakra governs our relationship with our own sexuality and the "birthing" of new ideas and creative endeavors.

Solar Plexus Chakra–Pancreas

The pancreas is behind the stomach and plays a crucial component in digestion and regulating blood sugar. We experience "butterflies" in the stomach when we are nervous about a new venture or doubting ourselves. The solar plexus chakra governs our self-esteem and is where we develop the courage to take risks.

Heart Chakra–Thymus

The heart chakra is the caretaker of love and relationships. The thymus lies in front of the heart and supports the immune system, the body's number one protector. The immune system is not affected only by physical or environmental triggers. Scientists now understand that healthy relationships and emotions support our immune response. When we are navigating heartbreak or emotional stress, the effects on our physical body and immune system can be measured.

Throat Chakra–Thyroid

The throat chakra is the center for sound, communication, and speech. The thyroid is found at the base of the throat. It regulates metabolism and can affect your respiratory system and heartbeat. When this chakra is overactive, we may talk excessively and rarely listen. When this chakra is sluggish, we might find complacency and sluggishness in the entire system.

Third Eye Chakra–Pituitary Gland

The third eye chakra is found between the eyebrows just above the bridge of the nose, and runs to the base of the skull, the location of the pituitary gland. If you touch the base of the skull and the center of the eyebrows/top of the nose, you will notice that they form a line from one to another. The pituitary gland is referred to as the "master gland" because it controls most of the body's hormonal and metabolic functions. The third eye is also the "master gland" of psychic abilities and intuition. The pituitary gland produces contractions during labor and stimulates the breasts to release milk during lactation. The early stages of motherhood are also a time when women experience high levels of intuitive insight and visualization.

Crown Chakra—Pineal Gland

The pineal gland lies deep within the brain and is responsible for regulating melatonin which controls sleep and the restfulness necessary to transport us to the dream world. The crown chakra is the center of dynamic thought and spiritual oneness which connects us to every living thing in the universe...as does the dreamworld.

The Seven-Year Cycles

Yogis believe these seven chakras develop in seven-year cycles starting from birth. Events that take place during these time periods affect the development of the chakra system and create blockages or freedom depending on the experiences.

Root Chakra: 1-7 years old

The root chakra is related to security, family, and survival. We are very dependent on family and caretakers to create a safe space for us to grow physically as we learn to use our voice, communicate our needs, and navigate our place in the world. We discover our likes, dislikes, joys, and fears in this cycle.

Sacral Chakra: 8-14

This chakra is all about creativity, emotional balance, and sexuality. We may experience our first crushes during this time, and hormones begin to make physical and emotional changes to the body. We are learning to communicate our physical and emotional needs with greater clarity and our relationship with our own sexuality is beginning here.

Solar Plexus Chakra: 15-21

The solar plexus chakra governs our sense of self and personal power. We begin to better understand who we are as humans through our interpersonal relationships. We develop dreams and goals which provide increased clarity about what we want out of life.

Heart Chakra: 22-28

The years of heart exploration often come with depths of love and heart-break in equal measures. The heart chakra governs our exploration of love for self and love for others. As we navigate our internal landscape with increased love and clarity, this may be when we begin to think about how we can make a difference for our planet and other people.

Throat Chakra: 29-35

The throat chakra is all about using our "big person voice" to share our needs, desires, and dreams. We are learning to communicate and developing new tools for self-expression. In this cycle, many people find and refine their true sense of purpose.

Third Eye Chakra: 36-42

The name of the third eye game is cultivating wisdom and refining our intuition. Many will have a deeper comprehension of the knowledge they have received in life and how to use it effectively. It is an amazing time to start or continue to develop a meditation and spiritual practice as we are at the gateway to the crown chakra which is all about spirituality.

Crown Chakra: 43-49

Hello mid-life crisis! This chakra's development connects us to a spiritual relationship with all of creation. This is when we may begin contemplating collective consciousness and our purpose for existing as a spiritual being. Blockages in this area may present themselves as having extensive thoughts about aging and death.

At 50, the chakra systems have fully developed, you have life all figured out, and you live happily ever after. The End.

If only! There is still work to be done, but now that the development of the chakra systems is complete, many of life's lessons can now be accompanied with more internal tools to use when traversing challenges and hardships. The work is never done, but the tools become more abundant as we stay committed to the path. Turning 50 is a big rebirth and an opportunity to start over. This will only happen ONCE in our lifetime unless we live to be 98, when it happens again!

Our lives pulsate in seven-year life cycles that correspond to the chakras. When we're 49 years old, we're in our 7-7 cycle—which is the highest (and air-iest) spiritual pinnacle possible. That means, the only way we can go at this point is DOWN—and that's exactly where we go—all the way, down, down, down into our 1-1 cycle where first chakra reigns supreme. After 50, we have an opportunity for a "do-over," but with so many extra tools!

Did you have a shitty childhood which negatively impacted your root chakra development? Do-over! Did awkward sexual development plague your early teen years? Do-over! Did your heart break in your 20s affect every other relationship after that? Do-over! Your 50s and beyond allow you to rework any of your past chakra development, AFTER the other chakras have been fully formed. This is an epic time of your life!

To dive even deeper into the chakra matrix, each of the seven-year cycles also ascends a chakra "ladder" that has a sub-chakra focus which correlates to an increased clarity and awareness or struggle and growth. The first year of every chakra cycle is a root year and the final year of every chakra cycle is a crown year *within* the chakra as it is developing. For example the solar plexus chakra governs our sense of self. So at age 15, the root chakra which governs adrenaline and our fight or flight response is the sub-chakra of our chakra that is developing our sense of who we are in the world. Teen angst, anyone? I'm not sure who you were at 15, but it makes sense to me!

Yogis believe that each of our seven chakras (chakra means "wheel" in Sanskrit) is a spinning wheel of energy that turns at its own set speed. When a particular chakra spins too quickly, we risk burning out. When a chakra is spinning sluggishly, we become stagnant in that area and our life.

When there is a blockage in one part of the system, all other parts of the system are affected. Remember those old school Christmas lights, where one bulb would burn out and the entire string of lights wouldn't work? Our chakra system works in a similar way. When there is a disruption at one point in the energy channel, the entire system is affected. When chakra systems are out of balance, they affect all aspects of our lives.

Chakra Meditation

I've recorded some amazing meditations for you so that you can completely drop into each chakra. You can find a sacral chakra clearing on our shaktirize website. However, because you have this book, I would love to send you over a complete chakra clearing meditation (as well as a few individually selected recorded meditations) as a gift. Please head to www.shaktirize.com/soulsurge and fill out our contact page. I'll send them over to your inbox as soon as I receive the request.

Moon Magic

KISSED BY THE SUN….GOVERNED BY THE MOON.

Have you ever been caught in a crashing wave? In Hawaii, you become familiar with the powerlessness and disorientation of being stuck in a wave's pull. As the wave rolls to the shore, you tumble around and around with it. Instinct tells you to fight and struggle to get out of the waves' natural pull, but every surfer knows that the key to your success in this situation is to remain calm.

Life is filled with cycles. The moon has its ebb and flow from fullness to shadow; the tides with its waves crash and recede in harmony with the moon's pull. Seasons change in a particular flow, and you too have your cycle. You can fight the changes, you can struggle and stay in a cycle, or you can surrender to grace and listen for the pull towards your salvation.

Women are lunar by nature. It is no coincidence that there are 28 days in both the moon and menstrual cycles. There are four cycles to the moon each 28 days: New Moon, Waxing Half Moon, Full Moon, and Waning Half Moon. Each offers us an opportunity to connect with ourselves and our purpose—to align with our destiny. Our bodies are incredible and have the ability to shed and purify each month through our menses cycles. During this process we can let go of emotions, fear, and the things that no longer serve us. The moon reminds us that we are cyclical by nature; we are inherently connected to the ocean's tides and the planet we live on. If we did allow OUR moon cycles to sync back up with THE moon's cycle, we would menstruate during the new moon and ovulate during the full moon.

New Moon

New moon is a time for weepy feelings. In native traditional cultures, women would take their "red tent time" during the new moon to bleed and release in community with one another. This was a very sacred time, not just for the women, but for the tribe as a whole. The visions, dreams, and intuitive ideas that came to the women during this time together are what largely dictated the cycle of the rest of the tribe in that particular month: when they hunted, when they migrated, and when they stayed put. We too can utilize this time to get clear on what our next creation or idea will be.

New Moons represent beginnings. They are for planting seeds and setting intentions for our dreams, goals, and wishes. They're an opportunity to take ownership for what you want to manifest and to commit to the actions, thoughts, and behaviors necessary to get you there. They're a time to give and receive—to form a community. The best time for making a fresh start and for beginning new projects is during the first two weeks of this new moon cycle. This is a beautiful time to draw in the life you want!

Trust the process. A life worth living doesn't always come easy, but life's lessons enhance your personal evolution. When you shift the story and view every obstacle as an opportunity, you have already begun to put your faith...in you. The most important relationship you will ever cultivate is with self, and when you have the faith to trust that the powers that be are leading YOU to your most divine purpose, you give yourself permission to get out of your own way and step into your divine power.

There are teachers for us EVERYWHERE, and even if they aren't always the lessons you want to learn at that moment, these moments contain undeniable magic. So trust the process. When the new moon is upon you and blankets you in darkness, it invites you to go inwards and embrace your shadow side. The new moon is also a beautiful reminder that the dark moments won't last. You are as cyclical as the moon, and you will once again rise to your bright and juicy fullness.

Sending you loads of love and sprinklings of shadows on this journey.

New Moon Ritual

You will need:

- A candle
- Dried flowers and/or essential oils (or a Lush sparkle bath bomb)
- A sage stick/incense/essential oil diffuser
- This book or a journal
- An open, receptive heart <3

Clean up your space a bit. A creative mind is best unearthed in a cozy and clean space.

Light your incense or sage stick and purify your place with positive intentions and blessings.

Take a bath or shower with your dried flowers, essential oils, and/or bath bomb. Listen to relaxing music or the sound of your heart beating underwater. Get comfortable.

After you have soaked for a while, slip into some comfortable clothes with a cup of tea and this book or your journal. Light your candle and get clear. Answer the following questions honestly:

What kind of life do you envision for yourself? Be specific. Write it down.

_____

_____

_____

_____

_____

What is your heart's deepest desire?

_____

_____

_____

_____

_____

_____

What is your "passion project," the thing that makes your heart sing and brings you so much joy to your life?

_____

_____

_____

_____

_____

What's the thing you love to do when you aren't working your daily grind? The thing you tell yourself you could never actually do for a living because it's "unrealistic" or "no one makes money doing it."

_____

_____

_____

_____

_____

**Slow. That. Roll. Beautiful.
Stay focused.**

Where did you learn the limits to your life? (Some of these belief systems were imposed on you even before birth!)

_____

_____

_____

_____

_____

_____

How can you use your one-of-a-kind skills to be in service to your world in a way that is uniquely you?

_____

_____

_____

_____

_____

_____

What if I told you that everything you desire in your heart was absolutely and totally attainable? You might think I'm full of it, yet I am living and breathing proof that when you commit to you, miracles happen. I am not the exception! There is nothing inside me that is greater or more special than anything inside you. But there is a catch: you have to stop believing everything _they_ say about you, and you have to get out of your own way. _Are you up for the challenge??_

Full Moon

When the moon is full, women are at their highest energetic point. Full moon is the perfect time for the outward expression of the seeds you planted during new moon time. If negative impressions were realized during new moon time, now is the optimal time to ritualistically release them. If you wrote your intentions down, this is the ideal time to do something bold to assert them.

Dance it out and let your energy flow during a full moon! This time is all about expression and being playful with yourself. This becomes even more amplified when you do so with other phenomenal females. Full moon is a time when a woman's energy is the strongest and most amplified. All of our ShaktiRize Wild Warrior Woman Weekends and teacher training programs are scheduled on full moon weekends so we can get down with our wild selves...together!

Full Moon Ritual

You will need:

- A disco ball, laser light, or something that makes your space feel more festive for the party you are about to have
- A playlist with your top 10 favorite jams
- Festive clothes you feel amazing in plus makeup and jewelry you love, if you wear them
- A pen and piece of paper
- Chocolate
- A bonfire (a candle in a bowl will work as well!)
- BONUS: Invite a few of your favorite people over to celebrate with you.

Light a bonfire or candle and sit in front of it or gather in a circle if you invited some friends.

Take a few deep breaths and think about the past two weeks (or two years if you haven't done this in a while).

Write down what you are ready to let go of. Be honest.

_____

_____

_____

_____

_____

_____

_____

Read those words aloud to yourself or your group. This may feel intimidating, but there is SO MUCH POWER in this step! The ability to bear witness and hold space for another woman is such a gift, and there is so much freedom in releasing these words aloud into the world before they are burned forever.

Say, "I surrender to the divine. I release my burdens. I am free."

Put your paper in the fire and watch it burn.

When all participants have finished, keep the lights low and pass out some chocolate.

Start your party playlist and dance until the sun comes up (or at least until your bedtime. ;-)

17

Soul Surge

I look back on my short 40 years living on this planet and sometimes I feel it all. I have seen sunsets that broke my heart more than any failed relationship...but in a good way. I have navigated relationships that left my heart feeling as beat down and breakable as earth-baked clay on a summer day...to the point of crumbling. Moments upon moments upon moments build a life.

There are the moments that brought me to happy tears and lit up the world in technicolor. There are moments that painted the entire world in constant shades of gray and left an aching in my soul. It's all part of life. It's good, it's complicated, it's magical and it can be fucking relentless.

You may experience moments when you are waiting to feel better, yet you are sad most days. These moments feel like a test. Can you withstand the sadness of each moment and trust that the change will come just before the sadness eats you alive? You hear you should not give up five minutes before the miracle happens, but it's deeper than that. It's truly a matter of life and death. Your life or your death. You have a choice.

When you are aching every day, waiting for a change...any change, it feels like there aren't any easy choices. Wait here in pain day by day, or cease to struggle by simply going to sleep and never waking up. Sometimes falling asleep forever feels like it would be so much easier. This is probably true. But when has taking the easy path brought the courage and strength you crave the most?

Life can feel like the worst sort of race. It's a race against time and a race against yourself. The clock is ticking and everything hurts. Are you going to feel hopeful before you lose all hope? Which will happen first? You succumb to the sadness and perish, or you start to feel a little better? When you are in the thick of it, you truly don't know. Each day is an agony, and staying in the skin you are in is torturous.

But what if a change is right around the corner? What if you wake up tomorrow and feel better? That tiny bit of hope keeps you going. Some days you do wake up and feel better. Some days you wake up so exhausted and heartbroken that just getting out of bed feels like a major accomplishment. Except in this race of life, they don't offer any medals for getting out of bed. They should. This being human is no joke. It's rugged, and it's not for the faint of heart. Can you dive deep into yourself and reclaim your strength before the sorrow consumes you? You have to try, because therein lies your magic.

Strength isn't something doled out at birth to unsuspecting recipients. It's not gifted to the uninitiated or unworthy. Strength is *earned* through moments of hardship and heartache that you see yourself through. It comes when you navigate your path through a valley of broken hearts, failed endeavors, and a river of tears to emerge victorious at the top, humbled but also miraculously stronger. We look with desire and envy at individuals who possess strength. We are unaware that these humans had to strip themselves to the bone to survive.

Strength comes at a great cost, but once it's earned, it can never be revoked. Your strength becomes forever intertwined with your soul self and levels up your consciousness for the next journey. You possess the ability to be stronger than you ever imagined. When life puts you through the fires of challenge and change, you have a choice: unearth those deep wells of untapped strength, or crumble and die.

These choices sound dramatic, but when the bottom drops out of your life, when you are alone facing your greatest hardship, when the world you adored shifts to something you never wanted, these are truly the only choices. To show up and live through it requires the greatest act of strength you will ever know. Some days just getting out of bed and brushing your teeth requires a warrior's courage. When feeding yourself is a monumental task and everything hurts, you keep fucking showing UP for it.

In those moments, YOU are my heroine.

I understand what it took for you to keep at it, to push through the pain and sorrow every day, until after weeks and weeks, it somehow felt a bit less incapacitating. You, my love, deserve an awards ceremony for your bravery, but instead you'll get a seemingly dismissive acknowledgment when people see you navigating hardship, "Oh, she's so strong. She can totally handle it."

Even in your aching, you make this personal growth shit look easy.

That's how strong you are.

I am so proud of you.

Being human is a gorgeous mess. It's filled with so many trials and triumphs, massive heartbreaks, and beautiful heart openers. We all do our best. We navigate the road of life with all our glorious limitations and the pounds of baggage that came to be ours by our mere existence. Some of these experiences are solely from this life, but sometimes it feels as if our heartaches existed even before birth. They feel as if we brought them in from many lifetimes before, as though we came into the world with an aching that refused to subside, no matter how hard we try to ease the ache.

Some are more fortunate than others, birthed into privilege based on class or color, giving them advantages over other people. Yet even with positions of privilege, they still fail to navigate the world with any more grace. Others come into the world with nothing but a promise and a smile, yet they find a way to juice from this life the sweetest experiences in spite of all the obstacles to overcome. Is there a rhyme or reason to this? Why is there still so much poverty in the world when there are simultaneously so many billionaires? Why do some people share the shirts off their back while others live in such a scarcity mindset they cannot even acknowledge their own privilege and power?

I have been both the giver of hope and the thief of dreams. I have been the one to ease someone's suffering, and I have been the one to create it. I have been a lover and a builder of worlds. I have been a manipulative destroyer of lives. I have been all these things, and most likely you have too.

The juxtaposition of being human allows us to touch the edge of heaven and the fires of hell simultaneously. This life carries with it so much elegance and so much destruction, and it is unabating. The allure of staying with it and overcoming these obstacles is that you get to experience it all.

Yogis believe that some part of ourselves signed up for this big, crazy mess. Maybe it's like a "choose your own adventure" book (remember those?). Your higher self chose the life you are leading with all its adventures, challenges, blessings, and setbacks to have THIS EXPERIENCE you are having right now. You knew everything that was available for you before you were even born, and you chose to have this life BECAUSE, not in spite of those things. Your soul self wanted to try this life on for size.

I'll stop for a moment to acknowledge that a part of this feels a bit like spiritual bypassing to me for humans in this world who are deeply suffering. To say that people have CHOSEN this experience in a past life also feels like victim blaming. I don't condone or advocate for either of these things. However, I have found when I am losing my faith in the face of adversity and uncertainty, part of me wants something real to hold onto, to take solace in the fact that *just maybe* my higher self was in for this crazy life all along.

As with all religion, spirituality, philosophy, and theories, there are few ways these things can be "proven," but beliefs are powerful. Your beliefs can change your thoughts which can change your actions and then the world. If you are able to hold onto an idea or belief that gives you hope in a tragic or uncertain time, that hope can supercharge your life so you can be in service to other people, help dismantle systems of oppression, or create solace for someone who is suffering. That hope may be the fuel you need to ignite the fire for change.

I had to shift my outlook, and I had to get back to my joy, and it has been/was/is, SO FUCKING HARD. It's hard because I am a human on this very complicated journey of life. The minutes that pass into hours and days and weeks go on for what feels like a joyless eternity. It can be so hard because when I am at the bottom, the middle, or even two inches from the bottom, it all seems like an impossible feat. To navigate out of any emotional pain or life trauma is a very personal and human journey, and it is not for the faint of heart.

All of this is made even more perplexing by the internal battle that reminds me that even though I am suffering, I am also very privileged. This may be a hard pill to swallow, but it's especially difficult for those of us who grew up poor, or unloved, or have experienced trauma. This is coupled with an insane amount of white guilt due to my white privilege, and a desire to change the world constantly. So when I was attempting to read some of the self-help books on life change, a part of me was on board and fully understood, but a part of me recognized the ENOR-MOUS GIFT I had of the means and ability to search for a place of peace. How do I simultaneously find a place of peace for myself in the world as a white woman, and also recognize that this in and of itself is a luxury? It's something that in the current moment, I still don't have the answers to entirely, but I do know that I can't give from an empty cup, nor can I be of effective service to others and the planet if I am sad, scared, or hurting.

To be of greater value to the planet and its people, you need to curate the value in yourself first, then share yourself with the world. So get your mind and heart right. Overcome your internal obstacles and start that dream career that brings financial abundance to your world.

Now the work starts. No one can get through it but you. You will wish for someone, something, some place that can create the shift your heart desperately craves. But no one will be able to stop the aching in the center of your heart where the pain is the deepest and your heart needs it the most. Not your husband, wife, or romantic partner. Not your mother, father, or children. Not your co-workers or friends. Only you have that power. In that way, when you are in the midst of an internal emotional, life-changing conflict, you will feel like both the prisoner and the imprisoned. You are jailed in your internal misery, but you are the only one who can set yourself free. When you are navigating the dark night of the soul, only you will know exactly what you need, but not how to get it.

You will need understanding and comprehension of your grief. You will need answers to your many questions and a reprieve from all the pain, sadness, and suffering you feel in the depths of your soul. You will need peace in place of the panic you feel every day. None of the people in your life will be able to give this to you in quite the way you need. You can try therapy, you can read books, you can change your lifestyle, and you can meditate. You can keep yourself busy every moment of every day, but none of these things will take away your heartbreak.

The only thing that can do that is time, the cruelest of currencies. When your days feel like weeks and the seconds feel like hours because of your internal aching, time is not a luxury you want to afford. And yet, it is a universal healer and change maker. With time, the jagged edges of rough rocky emotional terrain can become smooth and even beautiful.

Rather than this feeling like a depressing sentiment, my hope is that this gives you courage in the darkest of times. I hope it gives you a renewed faith in self that remembers that YOU, my love, have the power to create a deep internal shift. YOU are the one who can salvage yourself from the wreckage of your current existence, and you will be stronger, braver, and wiser BECAUSE of this internal navigation.

Even as I write this, I know that having faith in myself and my ability to transcend trauma when I am in the ugly, mucky thickness of my personal setback feels impossible at worst and unrealistic at best. EVERY.

SINGLE.TIME. I go through some major, groundbreaking life upheaval, I lose faith in my ability to transform myself.

"This time is different," I say. Even though I have seen the universe work its universal magic so many times in the past, there is a HUGE part of me (often the majority in these situations), that doubts a change for good will happen. A part of me believes *this time* my universal luck has run out, the karmic bank has been depleted, and my fortunes have permanently shifted. This is surely the time when the tragedy that is my life declines in a dramatic, downward sweeping spiral never to return to some semblance of normal (much less fortune), again. Even though universal law has proven itself to me 5,001 times, this particular situation is *clearly* different.

When I am feeling especially down, I can hear the story of my life narrated by David Attenborough as he chronicles the tale of a once self-less and kindhearted woman (obviously me), whose life unexpectedly and oh, so unfairly took a permanent and devastating turn for the worse, never to return to its former glory again.

Although there is still the possibility that my life could become an EPIC and tragic cross between a Lifetime movie and a tragic Shakespearean play...it hasn't happened yet. And the wisdom I gain from each of the challenging experiences I overcome tells me it won't. A giant part of me knows (as I am sure you do too) that these experiences will mold and shape me in a way that the happy and easygoing times cannot.

This life is both challenging and beautiful, with the same duality as the natural world. You are intrinsically a part of it all and interconnected to other people and every living thing on the planet. There will continue to be days that strip you raw with the amount of ache and sorrow they hold. There will also be days that take your breath away with the amount of abundance and joy they provide.

Life will always be good; life will always be filled with hardships; life will always be full of beauty. Stay the course of your heart's deepest desires and be kind to yourself in the process. Find how your own individual blend of magic can make the world more positive and hopeful for people everywhere.

Consider the Lao Tzu quote: "Water is fluid, soft, and yielding. But water will wear away rock, which is rigid and cannot yield. As a rule, whatever is fluid, soft, and yielding will overcome whatever is rigid and hard. This is another paradox: what is soft is strong."

In the Hawaiian language, there is a word for all water that is not salt water. It is *wai*. However, wai is so much more than just water flowing in a stream. The wai is the blood, sweat, and tears that flow through us and out of us. It is the water that rains down on our world and nourishes the land. When used as a verb, wai means something kept or earned, like the tears that flow through you during hardship, or the sweat you pour into your passion projects. Wai is essentially the cycle of water: rain, tears, sap from trees, and our connection to it all. It is all simply water, and we are simply a part of it all.

We must learn to be like water: fluid in the face of adversity, confident with the changing tides and shifting moons. We can be at ease in riverbeds and cascading from cliff faces, knowing that the curves and unexpected drops are what make us dazzling rather than cause our demise. If you can put your faith in that, sweet love, you will always flow into your own purpose and find the freedom your heart craves.

How are we going to inspire one another and our future generations of leaders if we aren't sure how the road was navigated prior to us? Early explorers needed courage to create the maps of old. They sailed to distant lands, then charted and uncharted everything as it was discovered and evolved. There is very little land on this planet that has yet to be explored, yet we have the opportunity to create new worlds within this one. As modern day explorers navigating the best paths for businesses, social change, internal understanding, and world issues, we are the courageous pioneers of some very uncharted territory; the maps of these territories are evolving constantly and some of them haven't even been written yet!

It is up to us to share the tricks and tools we have learned along the way and also the late nights and long cries that led us to where we are currently. The heart of a warrior is a humble heart that recognizes that so many things could have gone differently in our success stories. Only with luck, intuition, and a ton of grace from a higher power were we granted the place we reside in currently, and the knowledge that this position we find ourselves in is never "secure" or beyond reproach.

Be thankful for your struggles as they showed you your strength! Let the waves of change wash over your life and allow your soul to surge.

Real Talk Questions:

What do you want your job to look like?

_____

_____

_____

_____

_____

_____

What do you want your most intimate relationships to look like?

_____

_____

_____

_____

_____

_____

What do YOU look like? (Emotionally, physically, spiritually?)

_____

_____

_____

_____

_____

_____

How can you use this newfound understanding of self to positively impact the planet and its inhabitants?

_____

_____

_____

_____

_____

_____

How do you want to FEEL in a romantic relationship?

_____

_____

_____

_____

_____

_____

What nice things do you want to continue to do for yourself whether you are in a relationship or not?

_____

_____

_____

_____

_____

_____

18

Where to Go from Here

Now that you have unearthed some of your soul's sparkling gems, your work really begins. You see, it is one thing to dive into yourself to love yourself more as you evolve; however, a greater goal is to USE that newfound wisdom to create lasting social change and be in service to your fellow humans.

As an individual, you are strong, but when you join others for the greater good, you are infinitely, exponentially stronger. Your ultimate strength and power lies in your connection to your authentic self. It's that place of peace in the interaction of YOUR mind, YOUR body, and YOUR heart. It is not about being the "right" shape, size, or weight. It's living right within, so you can live right without. Learning to love, accept, and honor yourself also comes with the courage and responsibility to uplift and inspire others. How can you use your one, wild, beautiful life to be a part of the bigger change the world so desperately needs?

How can we, as women, use our strength to strengthen the greater good? After all, we are only as strong as the weakest member of our female collective. As long as there are women who are struggling, we have an opportunity to use our abundant resources to uplift our sisters around the globe.

Personally, I have always been passionate about women's rights, and especially global education for girls. I am a dedicated advocate for women's issues and am always looking for ways to dive deeper and support women on a global scale. I was curious to find ways that would *empower* women rather than put me in a position of *savior*. Micro loans are a powerful way to invest money into a woman who can build a business that helps support her entire community. Because the money is a loan, it stays in the lending system and can be re-distributed to other women in need.

Here are some organizations that support women through micro-loans:

- www.kiva.org
- https://poweroflove.org/projects/microloans-women

Another area I proactively support is education for girls. Sixty-two million girls are out of school globally and two thirds of the 792 million illiterate adults in the world are female. If all girls had a secondary education, 60% fewer girls under the age of 17 would become pregnant. If all women completed primary education, there would be 15% fewer child deaths worldwide.[12] If India enrolled 1% more girls in secondary school, its GDP would increase by $5.5 billion.[13]

When you educate a girl, they have a greater sense of their rights and more confidence and freedom to make positive choices. Education empowers women to overcome discrimination. Girls and young women who are educated are more than twice as likely to send their children to school.* Statistics show that when women earn an income, they reinvest 90% of their money back into families and their community.[14] When we educate a girl, there are so many more opportunities for global change.

Maybe your passion isn't in educating girls. That's fine! But do us all a favor and find what ignites the fire in your heart. See how you can use your individual blend of magic to positively contribute to the causes you support. Volunteer your time or donate money to organizations you feel

12 Source: https://en.unesco.org/gem-report/sites/default/files/Girls_fact_sheet.pdf
13 https://www.usaid.gov/girl/infographic-ripple-effect#:~:text=If%20India%20enrolled%201%25%20more%20girls%20in%20secondary%20school%2C%20their,She%20can%20increase%20her%20income.
14 https://www.un.org/en/ecosoc/phlntrpy/notes/clinton.pdf
Find out more:** https://www.womenone.org/

positively benefit your community. Actively work to fight the oppressive systems of white supremacy and patriarchy. Build the world you want to live in that extends beyond your own individual needs and desires.

Support people who are already actively doing the work. Rather than spearhead your own project, explore where you can help facilitate movement and growth in someone else's vision. There are plenty of nonprofit organizations and service-based businesses that align with your passion. Don't start something, end something. Get to the core of what you want to support and then rather than STARTING another organization, join someone and support them in your shared vision. However you do it, find a way to END systematic oppression, poverty, sexism, and racism in your communities.

Real Talk Questions:

The change I most desire to see in the world is...

_____

_____

_____

_____

_____

What ONE step can I take today to get closer to creating this change?

_____

_____

_____

_____

_____

_____

Having trouble? Start here:

I will donate $____ to _____ to support their mission.

I will donate my time and energy to _____

in the following ways_____

_____

_____.

You don't need to donate thousands of dollars or 40 hours per week to the cause you believe in (although that would be AMAZING and you would for sure get major karmic extra credit). Even the simplest changes can create giant ripples in the lives of many. Start small, and let whatever you share be from an authentic place, given with a humble heart. You are sharing yourself because you can, because it alleviates some sadness and stress in the world.

We don't support causes for the accolades or bragging rights at parties. We don't support other humans as a way to alleviate our guilt or "save" anyone. We are not here to be another's messiah. We are all humans on this path of life, and no amount of money, power, or circumstances make one person better than another on our soul's journey.

If you are new to this concept of sharing yourself, perhaps you could start by aligning yourself with an organization whose mission you support. There are plenty of amazing organizations who support every kind of need. But let me forewarn you that showing up in selfless service for the world and its inhabitants is contagious.

We must stay vigilant and focused. We cannot become complacent now and wait for someone else to build a future we desire for the world. It is up to all of us. We can do it.

Beautiful human, we CAN bring healing back to the planet and the people. We must be brave, honest, open, and giving. We must trust that the great power placed in our hands is within us for a divine reason. We need to move past our old stories of being non-threatening "goodie goodies" so we can share our gifts fully without apology.

Your world is waiting with bated breath for the things that ONLY YOU have to share. It is time to RISE up and serve all. Be the woman you are meant to be, not the woman you think you should be, or the woman other people expect you to be. Gaze at yourself in the mirror, and say "HEY THERE" to the beautiful warrior woman smiling back at you. Love her. Honor her. Cherish her. Unleash her into the world, with head held high, and allow her soul to surge!

Manufactured by Amazon.ca
Bolton, ON

25553091R00096